EDITORIAL RESEARCH REPORTS ON

CHALLENGES

FOR THE
1970s

Published by Congressional Quarterly, Inc.
1735 K Street, N.W.
Washington, D.C. 20006

Published January 1970

Library of Congress Catalogue Card Number 78-112448
Standard Book No. 87187-005-3

Editorial Research Reports
Editor Emeritus, Richard M. Boeckel
Editor, William B. Dickinson, Jr.

Contents

FOREWORD

THE DECADE of the 1970s stretches ahead like a vast, unspoiled prairie, waiting the imprint of man with all his follies, grandeur, vice, nobility, ignorance and ingenuity. The future is inscrutable—providentially so—and those who gaze into crystal balls must predict at their peril.

Nevertheless it is not hazarding too much to say that the 1970s surely will hold some nasty surprises for mankind. War and violence are eternal verities, and even the best of times bear their share of brutish behavior. It is cold comfort to consider that the conflicts and upheavals of the Sixties were, in the scale of history, modest bloodlettings.

We can more happily reflect on the slim but not impossible dream that modern man will begin to learn the hard lessons of history. One lesson, underscored in the decade just past, is that in the real world there are limits to technological and military power as devices for dominance and conquest. The Sixties were not kind to national leaders who forgot the advantages of humility and modest expectations.

We can forecast with some certainty that the Seventies will be more conscious of, and more frightened by, the youth of the times than any decade in this century. Youth is on the march in Europe as well as in the United States. Their advance is as certain as the goal is obscure. The children will do their thing, only more so, while older generations quake. Will this secular crusade lead toward a new and kinder day or toward a national nervous breakdown? We may know before 1980 rolls around.

The nine Editorial Research Reports printed in this volume explore a few of the countless issues that are likely to perplex the 3.5 billion people who inhabit Spaceship Earth as the 1970s unfold. A major difficulty, of course, is that we can anticipate problems only from the limited perspective of the present, knowing that our control of the future is inadequate and that the price of failure may be extinction. Travelers into the new decade should carry a keen intellect, strong nerves and—as the most vital baggage—a very large measure of sheer faith.

William B. Dickinson, Jr.
Editor

December 1969
Washington, D.C.

CHALLENGES FOR THE 1970s

by

Hoyt Gimlin

UNRESOLVED PROBLEMS OF COMING DECADE
National Social Ills in Prosperous America
Unfulfilled Negro Goals and the Urban Crisis
Racial Separation Between Cities and Suburbs
Policy Issues Here and Abroad After Viet Nam

THE SIXTIES: A DECADE OF RISING DISSENT
World Youth Unrest and U. S. Student Protest
Negro Revolution as Major Current of Dissent
Challenges to Theology and Church Authority
War Protest and Limits of Dissent in Democracy

SHAPE OF ACTION NEEDED IN YEARS AHEAD
Identification and Forecasting of Social Trends
Effective Measures to Protect the Environment
Changes in Patterns of Work and Leisure Habits
Control of Crime and Violence in United States

1 9 6 9
Nov. 19

CHALLENGES FOR THE 1970s

AMERICA enters the 1970s groping for new directions but still bearing the burdens of the previous decade. Trouble at home and abroad in the Sixties shattered many of the certainties with which that decade began. No period since the Depression Thirties has so undermined the country's self-confidence or been so hard on prophets and problem-solvers. "The Sixties posed problems, but the solutions to them were left up in the air," Michael Harrington has observed. "The Seventies will deal with them, or else." [1]

Americans hear almost daily that time is running out—to save the country from racial strife and the passions aroused by an unpopular war in Viet Nam; to save the cities from crime and decay; to save the world from pollution and over-population; to save themselves from the dehumanizing ills of an advancing age of technology. Yet they see prosperity all around them and share in it more than ever before. "We have heard nothing but despair and seen nothing but progress," Thomas Babington Macaulay, British historian, wrote in the 19th century. His words apply today but with a difference: "Progress" in 1969 has often meant a jetport which its neighbors did not want or an unneeded freeway through a park they tried to save. The most spectacular engineering triumph of the 1960s, and perhaps of all time, the manned moon landing, had its detractors. They asked why couldn't the billions spent on the space race have been applied to the social problems on earth. The 1960s, in short, were a time of change, dissent and upheaval.

NATIONAL SOCIAL ILLS IN PROSPEROUS AMERICA

Among the certainties of the year 1960, when John F. Kennedy vowed to get America "moving again," was that the ideology of class struggle had been muted. There was money enough for everyone, according to the neo-Keynesian theories of Kennedy's economic advisers, without taking any

---

[1] Michael Harrington, "Crisis of Affluence," *Center Magazine* (Center for the Study of Democratic Institutions, Santa Barbara, Calif.), September 1969, p. 47.

3

away from the rich. The key to their New Economics was to stimulate full production and full employment through planned deficits in the federal budget and through tax cuts. The Kennedy goal of reducing the unemployment rate to 3 per cent was never quite reached in the 1960s, but the spendable income of the average American rose by one-third even after allowing for higher taxes and inflation.

Gross National Product, the sum of all goods and services, almost doubled in the 10 years and approached $1 trillion as the decade drew to a close. But "G.N.P. has turned out to be a false god," Kermit Gordon, budget director for Presidents Kennedy and Johnson (1961-64), wrote in late 1968.

> In broad terms the economic goals of the 1960s have been achieved. . . . Yet . . . the mood of the nation is more troubled, and our internal problems seem more stubborn and incurable, than was the case a decade ago. The coexistence of growing affluence and growing social ills has led many to the conclusion that the vision of general prosperity as a solvent of social ills has been a chimera. . . .[2]

The growing affluence of the majority made the "Other America,"[3] that of slums and remaining poverty, all the more visible and troublesome. The Other American, typically, was a Negro living in a big-city ghetto, though he may well have been a white jobless miner half-hidden in the hollows of Appalachia. It is now agreed that both were victims of unfulfilled expectations in the 1960s. The promise of the War on Poverty never matched its rhetoric, in part because of the country's involvement in a real war in Viet Nam.

The economic record of the 1960s, though impressive, became badly marred by inflation. Guns and butter was the demand placed on the national economy by the Viet Nam war and the Great Society. The price was inflation. The Johnson administration failed to heed the terms of the classic dilemma—whether to buy guns for war or "butter" for domestic tranquillity—and decided it could have both. Most economists agree that the refusal to take precautionary measures of fiscal belt-tightening led directly to inflation. The intervention of inflation suggests how easy it is for economic plans to go awry.

---

[2] Kermit Gordon (president of Brookings Institution), introduction to *Agenda for the Nation* (1968), p. 5.

[3] Name derived from Michael Harrington's *The Other America: Poverty in the United States* (1962), a book said to have influenced President Kennedy's thinking and contributed ultimately to the birth of the Johnson administration's anti-poverty program.

The National Planning Association, a non-governmental group in Washington, foresees some slowing of inflation in 1970. The *Wall Street Journal* reported Sept. 30, 1969, that most of the leading economists it questioned thought the 1969 level of about 5 per cent inflation would soon decline. But none of them forecast a return, even by 1971, of anything like the "normal" inflation of about 1.2 per cent annually which prevailed in the early 1960s.

On the threshold of the new decade, there is fear in the business community of a "mini-recession" and higher employment—the price of the Nixon administration's "disinflation" program, one that employs the traditional tools of high interest rates and tight credit. For the entire 1970s, however, the National Planning Association has predicted that the G.N.P. will double again, to almost $2 trillion—if social disorders do not disrupt the economy.[4]

UNFULFILLED NEGRO GOALS AND THE URBAN CRISIS

Negroes improved their lot in the 1960s by almost every statistical standard and thus came closer to achieving economic parity with the white population. But the gains, however satisfying on a government chart, did not defuse the black anger which grew as the decade wore on. Any balance sheet is filled with "buts" and "on the other hands." Three of every 10 Negro families were earning $7,000 or more a year toward the end of the decade, twice as many as were doing so at its beginning, but average Negro family income was only 60 per cent as much as that of white families. Jobless rates for Negroes dropped during the decade but remained about twice as high as those of white workers. Negro students remained in school longer, but their achievement test scores continued to lag behind those of white students. More Negroes than ever voted in the late 1960s, but increasingly their demands were expressed through "confrontation politics" in the streets.

"The center of gravity of the civil rights movement has shifted almost imperceptibly from the South to northern cities," Dr. Kenneth B. Clark wrote in 1968. "The end of such patterns of southern segregation, long enforced by law and custom, was not relevant to the depressed predicament of the masses of Negroes who had migrated to the northern urban ghettos. Indeed, the civil rights victories won for the

---

[4] *Looking Ahead* (publication of National Planning Association), May 1969, p. 1.

southern Negro, limited though they were, were mocked by the fact that the northern Negro was required to send his children to de facto segregated and inferior schools and to live in racially segregated and often substandard housing." [5]

Less than a week after passage of the Voting Rights Act of 1965, rioting erupted in the predominantly black Watts section of Los Angeles. Six days of turmoil left 34 dead, 856 injured, and damage approaching $200 million. In succeeding summers, the nation watched the Negro neighborhoods of city after city consumed by burning, looting and shooting. The nation's capital itself was darkened by columns of black smoke for several days following the assassination in April 1968 of Martin Luther King Jr., the apostle of non-violent action in the civil rights movement.

The Kerner Commission warned that the country was "moving toward two societies, one black, one white—separate and unequal." [6] In one of the most controversial statements written during the 1960s, the commission asserted that "White racism is essentially responsible for the explosive mixture which has been accumulating in our cities since the end of World War II."

Since 1940 about four million Negroes have migrated from the rural South, most of them to the inner-city ghettos of the urban North. Ill trained for life in an industrial society, they have accounted for a great deal of the upward surge in the nation's welfare population—from 3.1 million in 1945 to 10.2 million today. In 1965, the Moynihan Report, as controversial as the Kerner Report was to become, emphasized the "deterioration of the fabric of Negro society" in urban ghettos, a condition it laid to the "deterioration of the Negro family." The report noted:

> Nearly a quarter of urban Negro marriages are dissolved; nearly one-quarter of Negro births are now illegitimate; as a consequence, almost one-fourth of Negro families are headed by females, and this breakdown of the Negro family has led to a startling increase in welfare dependency. [7]

---

[5] Dr. Kenneth B. Clark, "The Negro and the Urban Crisis," *Agenda for the Nation* (1968), pp. 117-118. Clark, a Negro, is professor of psychology at City College of the City University of New York.

[6] The National Advisory Commission on Civil Disorders, headed by Otto Kerner, former governor of Illinois, in reporting its findings to President Johnson, March 1, 1968.

[7] *The Negro Family: The Case for National Action*, written by a governmental task force headed by Daniel Patrick Moynihan, a sociologist and author who was then an Assistant Secretary of Labor in the Johnson administration and is now counselor to President Nixon on urban affairs. The report, written in 1965 for official use only, was made public in 1966 after some of its contents had been leaked to newsmen.

Challenges for the 1970s

POPULATION OF THE UNITED STATES

Year	Total *(in millions)*	Negro	Per cent Negro
1790	3.9	0.7	20
1860	31.5	4.4	14
1900	76.0	8.8	12
1940	131.7	12.9	10
1950	151.7	15.0	10
1960	180.0	18.9	11
1970*	204.9	22.8	11
1980*	227.6	28.0	12
1990*	255.9	35.0	13

* Census Bureau projections.

Moynihan found the "root of the problem" in slavery, in the effects of Reconstruction on the family and, particularly, on the position of the Negro man in an urban setting—the "last hired and first fired." He said the dimensions of this "tangle of pathology" were growing because of a relatively high fertility rate among Negroes.

Negroes make up 11 per cent of the total population but 15 per cent of children under five years old. In each of the two coming decades, according to demographic projections currently in favor, the Negro proportion of the total population will rise by a full percentage point.

RACIAL SEPARATION BETWEEN CITIES AND SUBURBS

Like other sectors of the population, Negroes have grown rapidly urban. They are no longer predominantly southern and rural. Americans, white and black, have been moving away from the countryside into sprawling metropolitan areas, which today contain 65 per cent of the population—a figure that may reach 75 per cent within five years. But while the Negro migration swept into the central cities, whites have left the city for the encircling suburbs. This trend has been under way since the 1940s, but in 1967 the Census Bureau detected something new. Whites began leaving the riot-prone inner cities faster than ever that year, but for the first time the Negro inflow dwindled to a trickle.

A polarization of the races was evident in the white outflow, but there was no clear explanation of why the Negro inflow dropped off so sharply. Conrad F. Taeuber, associate director of the Census Bureau, told Congress he was not sure

7

WHERE PEOPLE LIVE

(in percentages)

	Total population	Whites	Negroes
Central cities	29.4	26.2	54.0
Suburban rings	35.3	37.5	14.6
Non-metropolitan	35.4	36.3	31.4

SOURCE: Census Bureau 1968 estimates.

that it was only a "temporary aberration." [8] *Fortune* magazine had complained editorially a year earlier (August 1968) that "migrating Negroes are subjected to less study than migrating birds."

"With the growth of a black middle class of major proportions," Taeuber suggested, "we may find that more blacks, as well as whites, will shun the cities until they provide more of the kind of life people want." There is fragmentary evidence that Negroes are pushing into previously all-white suburbs in greater numbers each year. On the other hand, evidence is accumulating that the races on the whole are drawing further apart, a process speeded in the late 1960s by militant "black power" and a resulting "white backlash."

If the suburbs are indeed being opened more freely to Negroes, the inner cities will be left with the remainder of the black population, cut off not only from the white world but also from the Negro middle class. The prospect that big cities in the 1970s will be devoid of a middle class, white or black, leads mayors to speak of their problems in tones of despair.

"The cities probably will be the number one domestic problem of the 1970s," a news executive of United Press International, H. L. Stevenson, told a conference of editors and publishers in October 1969. Some urbanologists believe that suburbs are taking on a commercial life quite independent of the central city, thus leading the latter to wither and die. Alexander Ganz, an expert on city planning, has predicted that by 1985 the prevailing home-to-work pattern will be not from city to suburb but from suburb to suburb.[9]

---

[8] Testimony before House Committee on Banking and Currency, June 3, 1969. Taeuber said the average loss of white population in central cities during 1960-66 was 141,000 a year, while Negro replacements averaged 370,000 a year. Since then, the comparable figures have changed to 500,000 and 110,000, respectively.

[9] Alexander Ganz, "The Car is Here to Stay: Emerging Patterns of Urban Transport," *Technological Review*, January 1969, p. 33.

Projection of needs into the 1970s—for schools, roads, housing and a thousand other concerns—is especially important at a time when public debate is in the making over post-Viet Nam spending. Although the end of the war had not come into sight, it was clear by the latter half of 1969 that the Nixon administration was seeking to "wind down" the war—reduce the scale of the conflict and this country's participation in it. Even during Johnson's final year in the presidency, a new phrase—"peace dividend"—whetted the interest of congressmen, economists, governors and mayors. The phrase referred to cuts in military spending after the war and application of revenue thus released to social programs that had been "underfunded" or deferred during the war years. Estimates of the fiscal windfall ranged from zero to $8 billion and on up to $40 billion a year.[10]

POLICY ISSUES HERE AND ABROAD AFTER VIET NAM

Whatever the approximate sum—and indications are that it will be smaller rather than larger—estimates of its future allocation await determination of the nation's global role in the 1970s and hence the extent of its defense and foreign aid spending. The war created strong sentiment against keeping the United States indefinitely on duty as "world policeman." But it was by no means certain whether this sentiment represented majority thinking or whether it would prevail.

The Cold War struggle between the United States and the Soviet Union continued into the 1960s, but it no longer polarized the world. After the nuclear showdown between the two countries in the Cuban missile crisis of 1962, the Communist countries and the West both turned increasingly inward—to deal with the fissures and cracks developing in their own societies. Alastair Buchan, retiring director of the Institute for Strategic Studies, Britain's prestigious "think tank," said recently he foresaw no likelihood of global conflict within the next decade. However, he did predict some shifting of world power away from America and Russia toward China and Japan. At the same conference at which Buchan spoke,[11] the Deputy Leader of Britain's Conservative Party, Reginald Maudling, argued that a world trade recession in the 1970s was a real possibility unless the United

---

[10] See "Future of the U. S. Defense Economy," *E.R.R.*, 1969 Vol. II, pp. 711-728, and *Congressional Quarterly Weekly Report* of Oct. 24, 1969, pp. 2075-2088.

[11] In London, sponsored by the Westinghouse Broadcasting Co., as reported by John Tebbel, *Saturday Review*, Nov. 8, 1969, pp. 80-81.

States brought inflation under control and unless international monetary policies were made more flexible.

In focusing on America's foreign affairs for the coming decade, some leading scholars cast their ideas less in terms of an ongoing struggle between East and West than in terms of growing hostility between rich countries and poor countries. Two-thirds of the people on earth live in the Third World countries of Asia, Africa and Latin America, which possess only one-sixth of the global wealth. For the United States this uneven division portends increased friction with Latin America.[12] Past efforts to bridge the gap between "have" and "have not" nations have shown little success. Since January 1949, when President Truman launched the Point Four program of technical assistance to underdeveloped countries, the United States has channeled almost $40 billion in grants and loans to poor nations. In addition, since the United Nations Development Decade began in 1961, other industrial countries have contributed about $20 billion more in aid to the same areas. But now the Development Decade is being described as the Disillusionment Decade. In tacit acknowledgment of failure, the United Nations has called for a second development decade, the 1970s, amid warnings of impending Malthusian catastrophe.[13]

Shock waves of the world "population explosion" are reaching the shores of this country. The 19th decennial census, to be taken in April 1970, is expected to show a net increase of 25 million Americans, the most for any decade except the 1950s. Fifty years earlier, in 1920, the country's population was little more than half of what it will be in 1970. In November 1967 the total had reached 200 million; the next 100 million may be added by the year 2000.

Although the over-all rate of growth has been declining— to only about 1 per cent in 1968—more young people than ever will be reaching marriage and childbearing age within the next few years. Even if the birth rate continues to decline, as it has done since 1957,[14] the number of births will still be high. The 3.5 million babies born in 1968 would have seemed a great many before 1947, when the birth rate reached its postwar peak.

---

[12] See "Economic Nationalism in Latin America," *E.R.R.*, 1969 Vol. I, pp. 247-266, and "International Development Financing," *E.R.R.*, 1969 Vol. II, pp. 557-574.

[13] See "World Food Shortages," *E.R.R.*, 1965 Vol. II, pp. 543-562, and "Synthetic Foods," *E.R.R.*, 1968 Vol. II, pp. 885-900.

[14] See "Population Profile of the United States," *E.R.R.*, 1967 Vol. II, pp. 803-820.

The Sixties: A Decade of Rising Dissent

THE SIXTIES may well be labeled the Decade of Dissent. "Rarely in recent history," the Foreign Policy Association has observed, "has there been so much open opposition by so many to the established order, whatever and wherever it may be."[15] Protests erupted into violence in Berkeley and Peking, in Chicago and Mexico City, in Paris and Prague. The causes, when identifiable, differed from place to place. But wherever protest occurred, youth unrest was almost sure to be found.

Youthful Red Guards brought turmoil to China in their zeal for purifying the country's Communist ideology. Students in Mexico City embarrassed their government by rioting in the streets on the eve of the 1968 Olympic Games. Only months earlier, student-led demonstrations in Paris weakened the French government. Masses of war protesters, most of them young and many of them students, battled police in the streets of Chicago during the 1968 Democratic convention.

Student revolts in Western Europe and Latin America tended to protest the confining aspects of traditional university life, while in the United States there were additional reasons for campus unrest and upheaval. At American universities opposition to the war in Viet Nam and the draft combined with racial and education protests. Increasingly, protests took the form of direct action. Student sit-ins at the University of California at Berkeley in late 1964 brought mass arrests. From there the gospel of physical encounter spread to other campuses. It assumed a new dimension at Columbia University in April 1968 when radical and Negro student groups shut down the university by occupying key buildings for a week, until ejected by police in a bloody episode. A year later at Cornell University, black students displayed—but did not use—guns in their seizure of a building.

"The world seems to be full, today, of embattled students," George F. Kennan has remarked (*Democracy and the Student Left*, 1968). But, it is often asked, does it seem that way only because of a few dissidents and radicals? A Harris

---

[15] *Great Decisions 1969* (publication of Foreign Policy Association), p. 83.

poll in the spring of 1968 indicated that fewer than 2 per cent of the nation's seven million college students were "activists," and a Gallup poll that June indicated that only 20 per cent of undergraduates had ever engaged in protest activity. But *Fortune* magazine, reporting in January 1969 on the results of an attitude-research survey which it had commissioned on the country's campuses, said that perhaps two students in every five supported the ideas of a tiny but highly visible activist minority. On some issues—calling policemen onto campus was one—almost the entire student body tended to become "radicalized."

U. S. POPULATION BY AGE

	0-14	14-17	18-24	25-44	44-64	Over 65
			(in percentages)			
1960	29.4	6.2	8.9	26.2	20.1	9.2
1969	27.2	7.6	11.8	23.6	20.4	9.6

Median age: 27.4 years.
SOURCE: Census Bureau.

Except for outbursts by groups of black students, campus rebels have come from middle-class families. Their rebellion appears to be against middle-class, and typically American, values—values respected by the working class. Hence, the hostility of the working class to student rebels and the permissive culture they represent—that of drugs, long hair, nudity and obscenity. The student rebel is likely to answer that he is not "anti-American," that he wants his country to be true to its own ideals. He sees a yawning gap between national myth and reality.[16] The reformer who chooses to "stay within the system" has a radical counterpart who proclaims that hope lies only in destroying the system and building anew.

Toward the end of the decade there emerged, on the left, a protest against the whole sweep of American experience, at least according to the group's most ferocious spokesmen. "It stood in opposition not to particular injustices . . . but to the entire system, the entire, vaguely defined and virtually all-inclusive 'Establishment' . . . not only to the specific faults of America but to America itself, including its moral core, constitutional processes and liberal democracy." [17]

---

[16] See "American History: Reappraisal and Revision," *E.R.R.*, 1969 Vol. II, pp. 817-832, and "Universities and the Government," *E.R.R.*, 1968 Vol. I, pp. 21-40.

[17] William Lee Miller, "The New Anti-Americanism," *Center Magazine*, September 1969, p. 39.

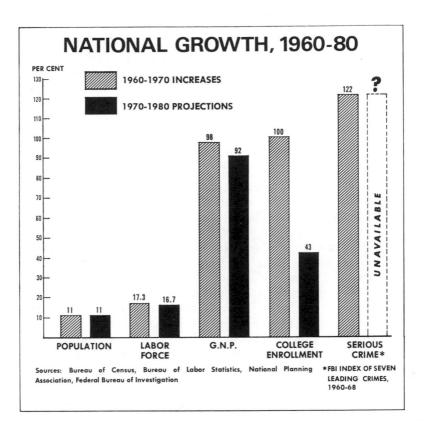

NATIONAL GROWTH, 1960-80

PER CENT

////// 1960-1970 INCREASES

■■■ 1970-1980 PROJECTIONS

	POPULATION	LABOR FORCE	G.N.P.	COLLEGE ENROLLMENT	SERIOUS CRIME*
1960-1970	11	17.3	98	100	122
1970-1980	11	16.7	92	43	?

UNAVAILABLE

Sources: Bureau of Census, Bureau of Labor Statistics, National Planning Association, Federal Bureau of Investigation

*FBI INDEX OF SEVEN LEADING CRIMES, 1960-68

Some social critics professed to see in the 1960s a return to the cultural protest of the Twenties, with its short-skirted flappers and gin drinkers, and to the political protest of the Thirties. Protest withered in World War II and failed to revive in the "silent Fifties." When it did revive, they say, there was a flood tide of pent-up emotion and anger.

NEGRO REVOLUTION AS MAJOR CURRENT OF DISSENT

The several currents of dissent, protest and radicalism in the 1960s tended to reinforce one another. Two main streams can be identified as youth restiveness and the Negro Revolution. Both were exacerbated by campus opposition to the war in Viet Nam. "Negro Revolution" is the phrase that came to describe what started as a civil rights movement that was basically middle-class, with the South its testing ground. Its objective was federal legislation in such fields as voting, public accommodations, education and housing. White people were welcomed to the movement.

13

The movement emphasized non-violence—the doctrine of its leader, Martin Luther King Jr.—from its inception during a bus boycott in Montgomery, Ala., in December 1955 through the lunch counter sit-ins and "freedom rides" of the early 1960s to the Birmingham demonstrations and the March on Washington in 1963. Congress passed the landmark Civil Rights Act in 1964 and followed with the Voting Rights Act of 1965. But the frustration of the Negro in the northern urban ghetto was not relieved.

By most reckoning, the high-water mark of the "old" civil rights movement came in 1963, but a new direction did not become visible until 1965, when a banner proclaiming the new words "black power" was raised in Jackson, Miss., to herald James Meredith's "March Against Fear" from Memphis, Tenn., to Jackson. The slogan became a rallying cry in the ghettos, though it meant different things to different people. To some it meant "black pride"—whether "Afro" garments and "natural" hair or cultural separation and economic self-sufficiency. As used in the angry rhetoric of militants, black power had menacing overtones—not only a rejection of integration and non-violence but an overt hostility to the white community.[18]

Dr. Clark contends that the extremists have only minimal support among Negroes and have been given undue attention by the news media.[19] Lerone Bennett Jr., a senior editor of *Ebony* magazine and professor of Black Studies at Northwestern University, maintains that the "black power" phase of what he calls the Black Rebellion is passing and that a new and still undefined phase is in the making. Huey P. Newton, a leader of the Black Panther Party, wrote in the August 1969 issue of *Ebony* that the black community was divided between "cultural nationalists and revolutionary nationalists." A cultural nationalist, he wrote, "seeks refuge by retreating to some ancient African behavior and culture" whereas the revolutionary nationalist—with whom Black Panthers identify—see no hope "as long as the bureaucratic capitalist is in control." Bennett asserted in the same issue of the magazine:

---

[18] See "Black Pride," *E.R.R.*, 1968 Vol. II, pp. 661-680, and "Negro Power Struggle," *E.R.R.*, 1968 Vol. I, pp. 121-140.

[19] Clark cites Kerner Commission findings and an Opinion Research study conducted for CBS News in mid-1968. The study reported that 1 per cent of the Negroes interviewed would give active support to Ron Karenga; 2 per cent to H. Rap Brown; 4 per cent to Stokely Carmichael, and 49 per cent to Ralph D. Abernathy, Dr. King's successor.

Challenges for the 1970s

Although it is too soon to say the final word about the Rebellion, it is not too soon to say that it is serious and that it is not likely to end soon. As a matter of fact, it is likely to get worse, particularly if the new President organizes a business-oriented, southern-oriented administration based on repression, tight money, and rugged individualism for the poor.

President Nixon has espoused the idea of "black capitalism" and on Nov. 6, 1969, his Secretary of Commerce, Maurice H. Stans, announced a plan to promote it. Stans said the government would make available $500 million in loans and grants by mid-1970 to help Negroes get started in business. Negro businessmen had complained that even with the government as co-signer, they were often unable to obtain loans from private banks. However, Stans' action was criticized in the black community as coming too late—more than nine months after Nixon took office—and offering too little.

No plan for transfer of wealth from the white to the black community has been so bold, or widely publicized, as James Foreman's demand for $500 million (later increased to $3 billion) from white churches and synagogues as "reparations" for centuries of white injustice to Negroes. The response of congregations has often reflected their division between activists who think that religion must involve itself in the social concerns of the day and traditionalists who think it should remain aloof.

CHALLENGES TO THEOLOGY AND CHURCH AUTHORITY

The church, no less than the state, suffered a "crisis of authority" in the Sixties. The Protestant world was churned up by a radical turn in theological debate in which the very existence of God was brought into question. Catholicism was buffeted by currents of reform unleashed by Vatican II.[20] Priests left their church by the score to marry, and the laity widely ignored a papal ban on use of birth control devices. Priests challenged the autocratic controls of the bishop's office, and the bishops in turn asserted a right to be heard in the church's decision-making councils in Rome.

A century ago Christian churches were shaken by new scientific discoveries concerning the origin of man. But the major denominations eventually solved the theological di-

[20] The Second Vatican Council opened Oct. 11, 1962, met for several months in the autumn of the three following years, and held its final session Dec. 8, 1965. See "Religion in Upheaval," E.R.R., 1967 Vol. I, pp. 3-19.

15

lemma with a minimum revision of dogma and ministerial custom. Today's upheaval goes deeper, coming from within the church rather than from agnostics and humanists. And it questions the relevance of Christianity itself.

Among Protestants, the "new theology" was exemplified by the titles of certain influential books published during the 1960s: *The Death of God* by George Vahanian, professor of religion at Syracuse University; *The Gospel of Christian Atheism* by Thomas J. J. Altizer, associate professor of religion at Emory University, Atlanta; *Honest to God* by John A. T. Robinson, Bishop of Woolwich, England; and *The Secular City* by Harvey Cox, a Baptist scholar on the faculty of the Harvard Divinity School.

Vahanian holds that Western man is "post-Christian" culturally and theologically; "faith," in the Biblical sense, is dead. He agrees with Nietzsche that once God is dead to the human mind and man is deified, man is more alone and estranged from himself than he ever was before. Paul Goodman, whose *Growing Up Absurd* (1958) was one of the best-read books on college campuses during the 1960s, dwells on the theme of alienation—which he defines as a Lutheran concept: "God has turned his face away, things have no meaning." Goodman compares the present with the year 1510 when Martin Luther went to Rome on the eve of the Reformation. Protest is everywhere now, Goodman wrote in 1969, "and the thrust of protest is not to give up science, technology, and civil institutions, but to purge them, humanize them, decentralize them. . . ."[21]

WAR PROTEST AND LIMITS OF DISSENT IN DEMOCRACY

What are the limits of protest and dissent in a free society? A democracy without the right to dissent is a contradiction in terms. Yet unless some limits are placed on dissent, and the manner in which it is exercised, a democratic government may give way to anarchy.

What happened in Chicago, in the streets of many cities and on countless college campuses, raised questions that go to the heart of the democratic process. Is dissent of any kind tolerable when the country is at war? Does the citizen owe his highest allegiance to the state or to his conscience?

---

[21] Paul Goodman, "The New Reformation," *New York Times Magazine,* Sept. 14, 1969, p. 150.

Americans have traditionally held that, in wartime, politics should stop at the water's edge and that the party in power should not repudiate its own leadership. The 1968 Democratic convention in Chicago demonstrated how far they had broken the first tradition and how near they came to breaking the second. An anti-war plank won 40 per cent of the delegate votes. "Never before in time of war against a foreign foe had so large a minority of a presidential nominating convention signified its readiness to repudiate its own leadership on so critical a question." [22]

President Johnson bowed out of the presidential race, March 31, 1968, in recognition of bitter division within the Democratic party and the country over the war. The President who stressed "consensus politics" and "reasoning together," who had won a landslide election victory in 1964 while promoting the Great Society, presided from 1966 onward over a nation more troubled by internal dissent than at any time since the Civil War. As the decade drew to a close, the protest movement demanded that the new Nixon administration withdraw immediately all U.S. troops from Viet Nam. An estimated 250,000 persons, predominantly youthful, on Nov. 15, 1969, mounted the largest mass march ever held in the nation's capital. The rally on the grounds of the Washington Monument was generally peaceful.

A recently published record of the Johnson years 1965-68 noted in its introduction that while extremists challenged traditional government processes, the great majority in the center felt uneasy over the apparent impotence of those processes. "Excessive faith in the national government may have been the tragic flaw" of the Johnson presidency, for "the reins of authority that appeared to be slipping from Washington's hands may never have been held there." [23] In keeping with Republican philosophy, and perhaps his own national pulse-taking, President Nixon has spoken repeatedly of returning to the states, cities and communities the decision-making powers that are "rightfully theirs." Plans such as revenue-sharing are sure to be heard from more fully in the 1970s.

---

[22] Foreign Policy Association, *op. cit.*, p. 84. See "Peace Movements in American Politics," *E.R.R.*, 1969 Vol. I, pp. 1-20, and "Protest Movements in Time of War," *E.R.R.*, 1966 Vol. I, pp. 141-160.

[23] *Congress and the Nation*, Vol. II (Congressional Quarterly publication, 1969), p. vi.

Shape of Action Needed in Years Ahead

AMERICANS can send men to the moon with reasonable assurance that they will arrive and return as planned. But "we are so ignorant about the functioning of society that we cannot set out to eliminate poverty, crime and air pollution . . . with reasonable assurance of success." This thought expressed by a sociologist, Frederick L. Bates, is echoed by a scientist, Jerome B. Wiesner, who contends that "The most important single need in our nation is to develop a more rational process for forecasting social trends and for developing plans to deal with the problems and needs that are identified." [24]

A committee of the National Academy of Sciences has urged the government to issue an "Annual Social Report to the Nation," and it has proposed that the President name social scientists to his staff of advisers. "We are living in a social crisis," the committee on behavioral and social sciences said in the opening lines of a report it issued Oct. 27, 1969, titled *The Behavioral and Social Sciences: Outlooks and Needs*. It explained the crisis as follows:

> There have been riots in our cities and in our universities. An unwanted war defies efforts to end it. Population expansion threatens to overwhelm our social institutions. Our advanced technology can destroy natural beauty and pollute the environment. . . . Even while scientific progress in biology and medicine helps to relieve pain and prolong life, it raises new problems relating to organ transplants, drugs that alter behavior, and the voluntary control of genetic inheritance.

A word that came into prominence during the Sixties and is sure to receive more notice in the Seventies is "ecology." It denotes a branch of science that concerns the interrelationship of organisms and their environment. If knowledge can be broadened, ecologists argue, makers of the pesticide DDT should realize that it would not only save crops from insects but also endanger the bald eagle, America's national bird, and leave a residue on food eaten by humans.

[24] Bates's remarks are printed in *Bulletin of the Atomic Scientists*, June 1969, and Wiesner's in *Technological Review*, January 1969. Both are adapted from speeches. Bates is professor of sociology and anthropology at the University of Georgia; Wiesner is provost of Massachusetts Institute of Technology and former science adviser to Presidents Kennedy and Johnson (1961-64).

Sir Julian Huxley, British biologist, believes that by 1980 technology may have far exceeded man's ability to control it. On this side of the Atlantic, Buckminster Fuller takes a more optimistic view of science and the future, but he acknowledges that mankind suffers because the "behavior of the whole is unpredicted by the behavior of the parts."[25] In short, humans are too frequently incapable of seeing beyond the immediate effects of their action.

EFFECTIVE MEASURES TO PROTECT THE ENVIRONMENT

When the returning lunar astronauts described to the people on earth the beauty of their planet as seen from afar, there followed a spate of speculation that man's awareness of his environment might be so heightened that he would finally try to halt what ecologists fear to be its slow destruction. They are saying in alarmed tones that the greatest danger to life on earth is not nuclear weaponry but pollution of the air and water from everyday living.

President Johnson described the situation in the United States when in November 1967 he signed the Air Quality Act into law: "We are pouring at least 130 million tons of poisons into the air each year. That is two-thirds of a ton for each man, woman and child in the United States. . . ." The act authorized the federal government to set standards for emissions from automobile and factory fuels. Together with federal aid to localities for sewage treatment facilities, it formed the basis for government action in the 1960s.

But money for these programs was in short supply late in the decade when inflation and the Viet Nam war imposed heavy cuts in domestic spending. A year after the Air Quality Act went into effect, its chief administrator, Dr. John Middleton, voiced concern lest its effect be nullified in the years ahead by increasing numbers of motor vehicles. "Today I'm afraid we're only making a small dent in a massive problem," he said. Middleton added that, at the present level of anti-pollution effort, there was little hope of cleaner air 10 years hence.[26]

City managers who attended the Brookings Institution's Urban Policy Conference in Berkeley, Calif., in June 1969 expressed the belief that by 1975-80 cities would benefit

---

[25] See "Science and Society," *E.R.R.*, 1969 Vol. II, pp. 775-791.

[26] John Middleton, "The Air We Breathe," *Population Bulletin* (publication of Population Reference Bureau), December 1968, p. 123.

from an "increased public awareness" of the need to control and prevent environmental pollution. They predicted that effective safeguards against air and water pollution would become increasingly important as a national goal.[27]

Even when old pollution problems are overcome, new ones tend to replace them. Pittsburgh solved its smoke problem only to be subjected to a new air pollution hazard, that of photochemical smog. Dr. LaMont C. Cole, an ecologist at Cornell University, has pointed out that 400 to 500 new chemical compounds are introduced each year, among them synthetic pesticides, plastics, antibiotics, radioisotopes and detergents—all posing novel disposal problems.

Aside from that, the sheer bulk of urban waste is taxing the ingenuity of disposal engineers. Philadelphia wants to ship its municipal wastes by rail to fill worked-out strip mines in northeastern Pennsylvania; Chicago converts some of its wastes into fertilizer and sells it to Florida citrus farmers. Waste abounds in an affluent society, John W. Gardner noted recently. "We are getting richer and richer in filthier and filthier communities," he said, "until we reach a final state of affluent misery." [28]

CHANGES IN PATTERNS OF WORK AND LEISURE HABITS

The age of technology takes a heavy toll of the human spirit quite aside from obscuring the sun and making parts of major cities virtually unlivable. The long-range change in the shape of work itself is considered a basic factor underlying youth discontent and protest. Those who are college-educated cannot look forward with confidence to jobs that will bring them independence, challenging work and social influence. "They can count on a fair measure of material comfort and security, but more and more youths are asking if that is a sufficient reward for the sacrificing of autonomy and growth." [29]

Labor leaders talk in terms of four-day and even three-day work-weeks in the 1970s, but American workmen have shown no knack for what Paul Goodman calls "serious

[27] *Public Management* (publication of International City Management Association) devotes its September 1969 issue to reports issued by the conference.

[28] Remarks to newsmen in New York, Oct. 8, 1969. Gardner, former Secretary of Health, Education and Welfare, now heads the Urban Coalition.

[29] John H. Schaar and Sheldon S. Wolin (professors at University of California at Berkeley), "Education and Technological Society," *New York Review of Books*, Oct. 9, 1969, pp. 5-6.

leisure." The *Harvard Business Review* calculated in its issue of May-June 1969 that factory workers actually had less leisure time in 1967 than in 1939. They were on the job an average of 40.6 hours in 1967, almost three hours more than in 1939, and their commutation time from home to factory and back had multiplied. The longer hours indicated a desire for more money to pay for increasingly complex and costly leisure-time pursuits.

Herman Kahn and Anthony J. Siener of the Hudson Institute "think tank" foresee a remarkably similar situation at the end of the century. In *The Year 2000,* they write that the lower middle-class worker will be earning $10,000 to $20,000 (in terms of 1965 dollars) in a year of brief work-weeks but "might still wish to increase income by moonlighting or by the wife's working."

It is instructive to recall that in 1960 automation was being portrayed as a producer of mass unemployment. Yet in the ensuing years of the decade, when automation was gaining its foothold in industry, 13 million men and women were added to the nation's work force.[30] Men lopped off the assembly line were needed in service jobs, including those of state and local government, whose number showed a dramatic growth. The serious displacement of workers came from mechanization on the farm, not automation of the factory. Machines made "corporation farming" possible and virtually eliminated the need for field hands. Mechanical cotton pickers and a dozen other labor-saving farm implements displaced sharecroppers and tenant farmers in droves. They migrated to the urban North and in many cases to big-city ghettos. Uneducated and ill trained for city jobs, they became candidates for welfare or crime.[31]

CONTROL OF CRIME AND VIOLENCE IN UNITED STATES

The ghetto has no monopoly on street crime, but it is a spawning ground. Urban crime rates tend to be highest in the inner city and to decrease as the distance from the inner

---

[30] An unpublished projection by the Bureau of Labor Statistics anticipates creation in the 1970s of an additional 15 million jobs, bringing the nation's work force to 100 million.

[31] Twenty-four million Americans aged 18 and over never learned enough reading, writing and arithmetic in school to hold even semi-skilled jobs, according to Dr. James E. Allen, U. S. Commissioner of Education. Allen told the State Boards of Education Sept. 22, 1969, at Los Angeles that the nation's schools should make it their goal to erase "functional illiteracy" by 1980. His office predicts that by 1975 automation will reduce unskilled laborers to 5 per cent of the work force, in contrast to 17 per cent today and 30 per cent a quarter-century ago.

city increases. The fear of crime and violence cuts across racial and geographic lines to become the "most emotionally charged" issue [32] in the 1968 presidential election. The F.B.I. Index of serious crimes rose 122 per cent from 1960 through 1968. One of the most quoted phrases of the decade was that of Negro militant H. Rap Brown, who told a rally in Washington, July 27, 1967, that "violence is as American as cherry pie." Three national leaders were felled by assassins' bullets —President Kennedy in 1963, his brother Sen. Robert F. Kennedy (D N.Y.) in 1968, and Martin Luther King in 1968.

The National Commission on Violence, appointed by President Johnson in the aftermath of Sen. Kennedy's slaying, recommended that presidential and vice presidential candidates make fewer public appearances to reduce the possibility of assassination. Dr. Milton S. Eisenhower, the chairman, said upon releasing the commission's report Nov. 3, 1969, that all political candidates should take the same precaution. Political assassination, he suggested, is not likely to diminish in the years ahead. The commission recommended doubling the $5 billion which it estimated was now being spent yearly to control crime. It was particularly critical of the system of criminal justice, especially the low quality of penal and correctional institutions. Similar criticism was voiced in the reports of the President's Crime Commission in February 1967 and of the Joint Commission on Correctional Manpower and Training in November 1969.

So it went in the late 1960s, a procession of study groups identifying the problems time and again—and making essentially the same recommendations for action. But for want of money or will, comprehensive action was deferred to the 1970s. If decades can be labeled—and there are those who say history cannot be neatly categorized at 10-year intervals—the Seventies are likely to become known as the Decade of Decision.

---

[32] So designated by the Gallup polling organization. See "Street Crime in America," *E.R.R.*, 1969 Vol. I, pp. 43-62, and "Violence in American Life," *E.R.R.*, 1968 Vol. I, pp. 407-423.

Science and Society

by

William Gerber

1 9 6 9
Oct. 15

SCIENCE AND SOCIETY

SCIENCE, long respected for its contributions to human well-being, is coming under increasing attack for allegedly debasing the quality of life. Criticism is especially intense among young people. Social critic Paul Goodman points out that "Dissident young people are saying that science is anti-life, it is a Calvinist obsession, it has been a weapon of white Europe to subjugate colored races, and scientific technology has manifestly become diabolical."[1] Such a viewpoint may be extreme, but it reflects the growing concern over the future role of science in a society which can land men on the moon but seemingly lacks answers to pressing human problems on earth.

Somewhat the same issue was discussed late last month by Samuel B. Gould, chancellor of the State University of New York, in a series of lectures at Colgate University on "The Academic Condition." The campus revolt, Gould said, "is against scientism as much as it is against authority." He explained: "It is an effort of the non-scientist, who has been put in the shade now for at least the past two decades, to get back some of the spotlight. Campus agitators are rarely, if ever, students or faculty from the scientific disciplines; they tend to come out of the social sciences, which are relatively inexact in their researches, and the humanities, which are and should be preoccupied with unanswerable questions."[2]

A special panel of the National Academy of Sciences, asked to appraise the benefits and drawbacks of technological innovation, reported on July 28, 1969, that the United States needed a new agency, close to the center of political power, to alert the nation to the perils of uncontrolled applications of science. The 17-member panel, whose report was commissioned by the House Committee on

---

[1] Paul Goodman, "The New Reformation," *New York Times Magazine*, Sept. 14, 1969, p. 33.

[2] Lectures at Colgate University, Hamilton, N. Y., Sept. 23, 24, 25, 1969.

Science and Astronautics, was headed by Harvey Brooks, dean of engineering and applied sciences at Harvard.

The report cited as dangers raised by unregulated applications of new knowledge "the specter of thermonuclear destruction; the tensions of congested cities; the hazards of a polluted and despoiled biosphere; the expanding arsenal of techniques for the surveillance and manipulation of private thought and behavior; the alienation of those who feel excluded from power in an increasingly technical civilization." [3] Rep. Emilio Q. Daddario (D Conn.), chairman of the House Science and Astronautics Subcommittee on Science, Research and Development, said the subcommittee would conduct hearings on the panel's findings.

British biologist Sir Julian Huxley recently warned that by the year 1980 man's mental aberrations may prevent him from handling the machines he has created and the polluted, overpopulated world in which he lives. The technology man has built, Huxley wrote in the London *Times*, Oct. 10, 1969, "has created a life of its own." By creating technology man is able to reach the moon, Huxley continued, "but through his Frankenstein tendency to let it outrun his powers of forethought and control he has imperiled the welfare of the earth and his own tenure on it." To handle all the intractable situations that will face man by 1980—overpopulation; waste disposal; air, water and food pollution; and other pressures on the environment—Huxley envisions a new breed of government bureaucrat or technocrat and the dumping of the bulk of the problems into the arms of government.

CHALLENGES IN LATEST SCIENTIFIC ACHIEVEMENTS

It is generally agreed that the accomplishments of science in association with technology, such as splitting of the atom and the moon landings, are showpieces of the human intellect. But the panelists appointed by the National Academy were aware that these accomplishments have potentialities for disaster as well as triumph. Disaster may spring particularly from disparity between the rapid progress achieved in the natural sciences and the slower progress, if any, in the sphere of morals. For science, although it creates a new world of options for man, does not ensure that the options will be used wisely.

---

[3] National Academy of Sciences, *Technology: Processes of Assessment and Choice* (1969), p. 1.

Science and Society

The outlook need not be gloomy, however, because the potentialities of science for good are as capable of exploitation as its potentialities for evil, and the warnings of evil issued by an agency of the kind proposed by the panelists conceivably might be heeded. Science, if properly applied, can go far to feed the hungry, clothe the jobless, provide housing, control disease, end illiteracy, cleanse the environment, and expand the horizons of human creativity. But to ensure that science will be applied to human betterment and not to destructive ends, to broader social justice and not to narrowly selfish goals, will require the best social intelligence that man can muster.

The challenge laid down by science to society, to turn the findings of research to beneficial ends through vision and sagacity, finds contemporary man ill at ease. The humiliating contrast between the victories of science and the mismanagement of human affairs was depicted recently by a newspaper editorial writer:

> For all his resplendent glory as he steps forth on another planet, man is still a pathetic figure, able to master outer space and yet unable to control his inner self; able to conquer new worlds yet unable to live in peace on this one; able to create miracles of science and yet unable properly to house and clothe and feed all his fellow men; able eventually to colonize an alien and hostile environment and yet increasingly unable to come to terms with the nurturing environment that is his home.[4]

The growth of scientific knowledge which is thus embarrassing the citizen is also creating problems for the scientist. Around 90 per cent of all the scientists that ever lived are alive today, and many of them are turning out new information. Over 50,000 scientific and technical journals annually publish about a million articles of importance for research and engineering in the physical and life sciences. Even scientists with a narrow specialty must run fast to keep up with new knowledge in their chosen field.

INTERACTION BETWEEN SCIENCE AND SOCIAL VALUES

Truths wrested from nature by scientific specialists may exert great influence on the standards and goals by which men live. This influence is felt sometimes slowly and sometimes with the impact of a swift kick. Scientific knowledge affects basic values in two ways: it may remove the underpinning from unsound beliefs, attitudes, and valuations; and

---

4 "Ad Astra," *New York Times*, July 21, 1969, p. 16.

27

it may open new vistas of what is worth striving for by making ends attainable which previously were only imagined or by making their attainment easier. In these ways, the truth can make man free by unchaining him from ignorance, prejudice and fear and by opening his eyes to a world of durable ideals and verities.

New scientific knowledge may alter accepted political, economic, or social standards or attitudes. John T. Edsall, professor of biochemistry, has cited an example of how the progress of science may change one's sense of what is, or ought to be, legal: "A polluted water supply was at one time an unpleasant but tolerated nuisance; when it became known that it was also a carrier of typhoid fever and other diseases, it became in effect a crime to tolerate such things." [5] In the economic and social spheres, technological marvels have converted what once were considered luxuries into "necessities" and transformed concepts of a decent level of living.

The influence of the social sciences on values is even more direct than that of the physical sciences. Maturing of economics, for example, undermined the high valuation previously placed on laissez-faire policies. In time, there developed widespread acceptance of the view that governments should intervene in the economy by promoting full employment, by managing currency in the interest of prosperity, and by adjusting tax policies to changing situations.

Science also has affected values in the sphere of personal conduct. Stoic attitudes toward pain, reinforced by the Puritan ethic, were undercut by discovery of anesthesia and pain-killing drugs. Growth of scientific knowledge about sex tended to liberalize attitudes toward relations between the sexes, birth control, and homosexuality. Traditional precepts on crime and punishment were weakened by John B. Watson's and Sigmund Freud's theories about the springs of human behavior. Scientific findings on smoking and health impelled many people to give up cigarettes.

The interaction between science and values is not one-directional. Ideologies and value judgments often have influenced the history of science. One need not be a Marxist to believe that economic and social conditions affect the world

---

[5] John T. Edsall (Harvard University), "Biology and Human Values," in Walter J. Ong (ed.), *Knowledge and the Future of Man* (1968), pp. 159-160.

of scholarship. Robert K. Merton, a non-Marxist sociologist, wrote two decades ago that "The thematics of science in seventeenth century Europe were in large part determined by the social structure of the time."[6] In the 20th century, ideological and nationalistic rivalry has been a causative factor in scientific activity, especially space exploration and nuclear development.

The mutual influence of science and values has bred one unhealthy feature—the blind worship of science, sometimes called scientism. A professor of physics wrote: "Among the signs of scientism are the habit of dividing all thought into two categories, up-to-date scientific knowledge and non-sense; the view that the mathematical sciences and the large nuclear laboratory offer the only permissible models for successfully employing the mind or organizing effort; and the identification of science with technology."[7] Walt Whitman gave an antidote for scientism in his poem about an astronomy lecture that was narrowly focused on diagrams and formulas. "How soon, unaccountable, I became tired and sick,/Till rising and gliding out, I wander'd off by myself/In the mystical moist night air, and from time to time,/Look'd up in perfect silence at the stars."

A reverse image of scientism is the anti-scientific posture of some of today's young people. Appalled at what science and technology have wrought in mass destruction, depersonalization and otherwise, they reject comforts provided by technology in favor of folkways leading to heightened consciousness and closer personal contact. Theodore Roszak, a history professor, reflects some of the disillusionment felt by youth in a science-oriented society in his book *The Making of a Counter Culture* (1969). "Under technocracy we become the most scientific of societies," he wrote. "Yet, like Kafka's K., men throughout the 'developed world' become more and more the bewildered dependents of inaccessible castles wherein inscrutable technicians conjure with their fate. . . . How does one take issue with the paternal beneficence of such technocratic Grand Inquisitors? Not only do they provide bread aplenty, but the bread is soft as floss: it takes no effort to chew, and yet is vitamin-enriched."

---

[6] Robert K. Merton, *Social Theory and Social Structure* (1949), p. 348.

[7] Gerald Holton (Harvard University), "Modern Science and the Intellectual Tradition," in Paul C. Obler and Herman A. Estrin (eds.), *The New Scientist; Essays on the Methods and Values of Modern Science* (1962), pp. 31-32.

Doubts about the value of science are felt not only by young people. They are expressed also by many adults especially in discussions of the federal budget. Charles Evers, Negro mayor of Fayette, Miss., said on July 21, 1969: "Before one more dollar is spent on outer space, we must make sure that not one child here on earth goes to a dinner table with no food on it." Feeding hungry children may be entitled to as high a priority in allocation of public expenditures as any other activity, but whether science should be deprived of funds until all deserving welfare objectives have been met is a different question.

COMPETITORS IN THE FIGHT FOR BUDGET DOLLARS

American scientists already feel that certain government-financed science budgets are at a low level. A combination of cuts, hold-downs and inflation has meant a 20 per cent cut in the last two years in academic research—basic and advanced studies at universities, hospitals and similar centers. The Washington *Post* reported on Oct. 13, 1969, that in many scientific fields this meant a more than 40 per cent cut since fiscal 1967, the year science budgets began leveling off. The *Post* quoted an unidentified scientist as saying: "We are witnessing a mindless dismantling of the American scientific enterprise."

The claim of science for government funds derives support from diverse considerations. At one level, basic research helps to fulfill the desire of man to understand the world into which he has been born. At another level, science enables practical men to apply new truths in the service of humanity. On a crasser level, science may become a symbol of political superiority. In this game, Sputnik scored for the Russians, the moon walk for the Americans.[8]

Whether nations can afford adequate expenditures for science as well as social justice depends in part on decisions concerning military budgets. Defense ranks near the top among all claimants for the public dollar, and in some respects the military establishment acts as an ally of science in the budget competition by steadily pressing the case for new weapons systems. As for the independent claims of science and of social justice, the main questions in this

---

[8] A professor of international relations observed recently that "The world is crying out for bread and is being offered moondust."—Lord Ritchie-Calder (University of Edinburgh), "Moonshot—The Great Diversion," *New York Times*, July 19, 1969, p. 24. See "Goals in Space," *E.R.R.*, 1968 Vol. II, pp. 832-837 and 841-842.

country at the moment are: When the war in Viet Nam, or American participation in that war on the present scale, comes to an end, will it be possible to make substantial reductions in military spending? Will arms talks with the Soviet Union likewise make possible a reduction of the arms burden?[9] And, most important, will Congress be willing to divert to scientific and social expenditures the bulk of any "peace dividend" that may be realized?

The Bureau of the Budget in the summer of 1969 examined the probable effect of peace in Viet Nam on the availability of funds for welfare, advancement of science, and other purposes. Daniel P. Moynihan, executive secretary of the President's Urban Affairs Council, interpreted the Bureau's report to indicate that the peace dividend would be absorbed by normal budgetary increases. Other White House aides rejected that interpretation. The President himself took a middle position, stating in an address on Sept. 1, 1969, at the National Governors' Conference, Colorado Springs: "There should be no illusion that what some call the 'peace and growth dividend' will automatically solve our national problems, or release us from the need to establish priorities."

SCIENCE AND POLLUTION OF HUMAN ENVIRONMENT

Science and expediency compete not only in budget-making but also in programs for utilizing the environment. The natural environment of man, on which he depends for his most basic needs, includes land and minerals, water and air, plants and animals. His social environment includes his habitation, neighborhood, and recreation areas; his family, friends, and associates; and the social and political institutions in which he participates or which affect him. The extraordinary extent to which man can modify his environment is one of the features distinguishing him from other animals.

However, with the aid of scientific inventions or processes, man often has acted irresponsibly in his treatment of the environment. He has polluted the air and water with industrial wastes and exhaust fumes, dumped litter where it did not belong, raped the soil and forest lands, hunted animals to near-extinction, harmed useful animals and plants by spraying chemicals in ways which seriously disturb the

---

[9] See "Prospects for Arms Control," *E.R.R.*, 1969 Vol. I, pp. 269-270.

balance of nature, and overcrowded cities and highways. René Dubos, professor of environmental medicine, wrote early this year: "The man of flesh and bone will not be impressed by the fact that a few of his contemporaries can explore the moon, program their dreams, or use robots as slaves, . . . if he has to watch [these acrobatics] with his feet deep in garbage and with smog in his eyes." [10]

There is small comfort in knowing that in some ways pollution was once even worse than it is now. A California biologist has observed:

> People who complain of the increasing pollution of the air never saw England's industrial Midlands, so appropriately named the "Black Country," early in this century or even Pittsburgh in the 1930s. Viewed on this time scale, air pollution has been strikingly decreased. . . . As for water pollution, in the middle of the last century one drank unboiled water at one's peril, and indeed in eastern Europe and Asia one still does; . . . Safe drinking water for city dwellers is a relatively recent gain for civilization.[11]

Although the improvements described are genuine, the need for new controls has increased with the growth of population, migration to the cities, the proliferation of motor vehicles, and the general increase of industrial production. Congress has taken cognizance of the problem by passing five anti-pollution laws.[12] But only a year ago, on Oct. 24, 1968, Richard D. Vaughan, chief of the Solid Waste Program of the U. S. Public Health Service reported serious inadequacies in 94 per cent of existing dump operations in the United States and in 75 per cent of incinerator operations.

Steps in Putting Science to Man's Use

THE LAG between man's knowledge and his moral responsibility is not a new phenomenon. As Arnold J. Toynbee has noted, "We have been living with this dangerous incongruity between our ethics and our power ever since we became human." [13] But the gap has become wider over the course of

---

[10] René Dubos (Rockefeller University), "Is This Progress—or Self-Destruction?" *New York Times*, Jan. 6, 1969, p. 142.

[11] Kenneth V. Thimann (University of California at Santa Cruz), "Science as an Instrument of Service," *Science*, May 30, 1969, p. 1013.

[12] Air Pollution Act of 1955, Clean Air Act of 1963, Water Quality Act of 1965, Solid Waste Disposal Act of 1965, and Air Quality Act of 1967.

[13] Arnold J. Toynbee, *Science in Human Affairs; An Historian's View* (1968), p. 7.

many generations. Taming of fire, development of agriculture and metallurgy, and invention of the wheel and the arrow immeasurably increased man's potentialities for constructive and destructive action.

Stimulation of science by social needs was manifest from an early period. In the countries bordering the eastern Mediterranean, development of rights in land led to techniques of surveying and theorems of geometry; commerce led to mathematics, accounting, and writing; urban society led to architecture; and the needs of civilization led to the calendar, astronomy, geography, and navigation. Similar developments occurred in India, China, and elsewhere.

The Greeks conceived the idea that the cosmos operates in accordance with rational laws. This abstract idea had a social counterpart. Knowledge of the laws of the universe, the Greeks felt, implied arrogance, which the gods would not tolerate. Zeus, the myth-makers said, punished Prometheus for teaching man the use of fire and also punished man, for man's part in the offense, by releasing evils from Pandora's Box. Summarizing the ambiguous social consequences of science, Sophocles wrote in *Antigone:* "He [man] has learned speech and wind-swift thought, and how to live in cities and to shelter from the bite of frost and the lash of sleet. . . . Baffled by no emergency, possessing by his skill resources beyond belief, sometimes he comes to harm, sometimes to prosperity."

Greek achievements in theoretical science in the fourth century B.C. included Aristotle's logic, his reports on animal physiology, and his geared-wheels theory of planetary movements. Among later Greek scientific landmarks were Euclid's geometry, Archimedes' doctrine of levers, and Ptolemy's elaboration of Aristotle's theories on the movement of heavenly bodies. Greek scientists belittled social applications of their theories. Technical work, in their opinion, was the responsibility of uneducated craftsmen.

LACK OF A THIRST FOR TRUTH IN THE DARK AGES

Rome translated the principles of order learned from Greece to a social domain, that of administration. In law codes especially, Rome reached a historic peak of excellence. Its application of standards of administration to physical aspects of civilization led to unexcelled construction of roads and aqueducts throughout the period of Roman hegemony and to an astute definition of the principles of architecture by Vitruvius in the first pre-Christian century.

The Teuton invasions, the fall of Rome, and transfer of the center of cultural life to Byzantium were followed by a decline in the thirst for knowledge of the principles which govern the physical universe. Little progress was made in any of the practical sciences during the first millennium of the Christian era. Although recent historians reject the view that the so-called Dark Ages were wholly unenlightened, the period was barren of epochal advances in knowledge.

Political power was decentralized after the fall of Rome and again after the breakup of Charlemagne's empire. This decentralization, taken together with such factors as stagnation in methods of transportation and communication, contributed to evolution of a new system of social standards and institutions—feudalism. Within that system, two technological inventions of the eighth century, the stirrup and the iron horseshoe, had a major effect on military budgets. These new devices made mounted troops a virtual necessity for victory on the battlefield. But mounted troops were more expensive to maintain than foot soldiers. The increased cost was reflected in levies on tenants, burghers, and others.

REBORN SCIENCE AND THE INDUSTRIAL REVOLUTION

Beginning with the Renaissance, a series of scientific ideas and discoveries shook the foundations of society. Copernicus defied the authority of Aristotle, the Bible, and the church fathers when he propounded the theory that the sun, rather than the earth, was the central body around which the planets revolved. Francis Bacon, preaching the doctrine of power through knowledge, challenged the rulers of Christendom to raise the living standards of whole societies by application of scientific theories.

Galileo later antagonized the leaders of the Inquisition with his advocacy of the Copernican view. "Many theologians felt that the Copernican astronomy was so clearly incompatible with the Bible," writes historian Will Durant, "that if it prevailed the Bible would lose authority and Christianity itself would suffer." [14] On March 5, 1616, the Holy Office at the Vatican published its historic edict: "The view that the sun stands motionless at the center of the

---

[14] Will Durant, *The Age of Reason Begins: The Story of Civilization—Part VII* (1961), p. 606.

universe is foolish, philosophically false, and utterly heretical, because contrary to Holy Scripture."

The Inquisition in 1633 pronounced Galileo guilty of heresy. He was made to kneel, repudiate the Copernican theory, and was put under house arrest for life. On Jan. 8, 1642, age 77, he died in the arms of his disciples. In 1835 the Catholic Church finally withdrew the works of Galileo from her Index of Prohibited Books.

Newton's formulation of the law of gravitation and the laws of motion; the answer of Laplace, French astronomer and mathematician, to Napoleon's question on the place of God in the scientific explanation of the solar system ("Sire, I have no need of that hypothesis") ; and Darwin's marshaling of the evidence for evolution of man from other species— all were traumatic in their effect on fundamental beliefs held throughout the world in recent centuries. Warfare between science and religion flared repeatedly. Only recently have these two opponents reached a measure of agreement based on the principle that each has legitimate claim to an area where it may remain supreme.

Meanwhile, widespread use of the steam engine and innovations in production machinery, utilizing scientific principles, brought on a revolution in industry of enormous benefit to mankind, though for too many years at the expense of exploited child and adult factory labor. Improvements in navigation during the same period promoted world trade and, at the same time, colonial conquest and exploitation. Henry Adams, in a letter of April 11, 1862, to his brother Charles Francis, wrote: "Man has mounted science, and is now run away with. I firmly believe that before many centuries more, science will be the master of man. The engines he will have invented will be beyond his strength to control." [15]

REVIEW OF VALUES IN WAKE OF THE ATOM BOMB

Whether the engines invented by man have reached a point beyond his capacity to control was one of the grave questions posed by the explosion of atomic bombs in 1945. Before the bombs were dropped on Hiroshima and Nagasaki, a group of atomic scientists had petitioned President Truman to arrange for a demonstration explosion in the Pacific

---

[15] Worthington C. Ford (ed.), *A Cycle of Adams Letters, 1861-1865* (1920), Vol. I, p. 135.

area to warn Japan and the world of the potency of the new weapon. But the President did not believe that such a demonstration would induce Japan to surrender. J. Robert Oppenheimer, director of the Los Alamos laboratory, reportedly said in August 1945, after the bombs were dropped, that "Science has at last known sin."

The *Bulletin of the Atomic Scientists*, founded in 1945, became a vehicle for reexamination of the relations of science to society. This periodical frequently has emphasized the dangers in failure to agree on controlled disarmament. The World Federation of Scientific Workers was set up in London in 1946, with Communist sympathizer Frédéric Joliot-Curie as its first president, "to ensure that science is applied to help solve the urgent problems of the time." The federation now has national affiliates in the United States and 20 other countries, including Communist countries. Atomic scientists, Edward Teller wrote in 1947, have a double duty: (1) to help produce atomic bombs as long as a threat of war exists and (2) "to work for a world government which alone can give us freedom and peace." [16] Linus Pauling, a scientist who later became an opponent of Teller's views on continuing production of atomic bombs, in 1949 promoted establishment of the Society for Social Responsibility in Science, which today has members in 25 countries. [17]

Referring to the 1940s, Anatol Rapoport, a mathematical biologist, has written: "The view of the scientist as a mere technician without responsibility for the consequences of his contributions was explicitly rejected by many scientists. This view had a much too disturbing resemblance to the justifications offered by the defendants of the Nuremberg trials." [18] Growing awareness of the interactions of science and government was influential in the establishment by Congress in 1950 of the National Science Foundation, in the appointment by President Eisenhower in 1958 of a Special Assistant for Science and Technology, and in expansion of the National Institutes of Health to the point of becoming the principal supporter of biological and medical sciences in the world. [19]

[16] Quoted in Morton Grodzins and Eugene Rabinowitch (eds.), *The Atomic Age; Scientists in National and World Affairs* (1963), p. 124.

[17] Pauling won two Nobel prizes, in chemistry (1954) and peace (1962).

[18] Anatol Rapoport (University of Michigan), "The Scientist's Social Responsibility," *Michigan Quarterly Review,* Summer 1968, p. 171.

[19] See "National Science Policy," *E.R.R.,* 1960 Vol. I, pp. 364-365, 368-369, and "Government Research and Development," *E.R.R.,* 1962 Vol. I, pp. 41-60.

Science and Society

Albert Einstein, Bertrand Russell, and eight other scientists and intellectuals, disturbed over the possible use of hydrogen bombs in war, issued a call in 1955 for a nongovernmental international conference on the social implications of science. The sponsors accepted the invitation of Cyrus S. Eaton, a Cleveland businessman, to use his home at Pugwash, Nova Scotia, as the conference site. That conference, in July 1957, was followed by other "Pugwash conferences," held annually in various American and European cities, including Moscow. In 1964, the International Business Machines Corp. established a Program on Technology and Society at Harvard University, with a $5 million grant, to study the impact of technology on employment, leisure, values, economic organization, health, and other aspects of social and political life.

A number of thinkers interested in the interrelations of science and ethics were prompted to try to determine whether any valid inferences could be drawn from knowledge of what is to knowledge of what ought to be. According to Harold Urey, professor of chemistry at the University of California at San Diego, scientific discovery shows only that some things must be so and must be believed but not that any specific conduct is right: "Science . . . never imposes a condition represented by the word *ought.*" [20]

However, an eminent British neurologist, Lord Brain, sought to derive a definite political precept from the same starting point: "Science . . . has a morality of its own, the foundation of which is respect for truth, and which, therefore, is bound to come in conflict with all attempts to curb freedom of thought and speech by any form of authoritarianism." [21] Paul W. Kurtz, a leader of the philosophical movement known as humanism, went further, asserting that knowledge of human desire for security, growth, love, understanding, and creativity, although it is "only one among many tests for a decision," nevertheless has a compelling force in the choice of values: "Once we have such knowledge of human nature it is not easy to ignore it." [22]

---

[20] Harold Urey, "Society and Science," in *The Impact of Science* (proceedings of a conference sponsored by the University of California at San Diego in 1963), p. 17. Urey won the Nobel prize in chemistry in 1934.

[21] Walter R. Brain, *Science and Man* (1966), p. 105.

[22] Paul W. Kurtz (State University of New York at Buffalo), *Decision and the Condition of Man* (1965), p. 246.

Links of Science and Society in Future

SOCIALLY ORIENTED scientific activities in recent years suggest that the scientist's sense of social responsibility is growing. Wilbur J. Cohen, outgoing Secretary of Health, Education, and Welfare, on Jan. 19, 1969, issued a 198-page document entitled *Toward a Social Report,*[23] which he hoped would lead to publication by the government of an annual report on social conditions and problems, corresponding to the annual Economic Report of the President required by the Employment Act of 1946. Behind the proposal for an annual social report was the theory that social scientists in the government have a responsibility to point out social needs which public and private resources should be mobilized to meet.[24]

A large number of research scientists at the Massachusetts Institute of Technology and other academic institutions conducted a work stoppage on March 4, 1969, leaving their laboratories to participate in discussions of the bearing of science on public affairs. A demonstration associated with the work stoppage was directed mainly against the war in Viet Nam and installation of an anti-ballistic missile system. At London the following month, approximately 200 scientists, including 10 Nobel laureates, founded a British Society for Social Responsibility in Science, complementing the society founded by Pauling in the United States 20 years ago.

Sidney Hyman has pointed to one of the possible disadvantages of encouraging scientists to discuss public issues. "The expertness of a man in the theoretical or applied sciences," he said, "guarantees nothing else about him, not his moral integrity, not his emotional discipline, not his power of social invention, nor his title of right to guide the political process in matters beyond his own special field." [25] However, scientists are uniquely qualified, within the compass of their specialties, to give valuable advice on the

[23] Containing statistical and analytical data on health, life expectancy, social mobility, the physical environment, waste disposal, income and poverty, public order and safety, learning, science, art, participation, and alienation.

[24] Walter F. Mondale (D Minn.) and 20 other senators on Jan. 15, 1969, introduced a bill (S. 5) providing for appointment of a Council of Social Advisers and issuance of an annual social report. Rep. Claude D. Pepper (D Fla.) said on March 25 that he would support such a bill in the House.

[25] Sidney Hyman, "How Do We Know Which Scientific Expert to Believe?" *Washington Post,* Aug. 17, 1969, p. B1.

effectiveness of alternative technical means of tackling such problems as air and water pollution, crime control and drug addiction.

METHODS OF DISTRIBUTING THE FRUITS OF SCIENCE

Exploration of the means of achieving social goals on which there is agreement is a prime need of the present era. Yet, in the opinion of Henry W. Riecken, president of the Social Science Research Council, "except in very limited or spotty areas, social development or social engineering does not exist." [26] Society is at last in a position, technically, to produce enough food, clothing, shelter, schools, teaching materials, medicines and other goods for the population of the world at its present level. But knowing how to produce the goods is not enough. More effective political and social policies are required to get them into the possession of individuals, families, and communities that want them.

Economic planning by public officials, once condemned as violating the natural order of society, is now widely acknowledged to be salutary. Emmanuel G. Mesthene, executive director of Harvard's Program on Technology and Society, favors a system of social planning which would complement the market economy. He cites in support of his proposal the fact that pollution and similar problems "are with us in large measure because it has not been anybody's explicit business to foresee and anticipate them." [27]

The United States has adopted, through Medicare and Medicaid, limited socialization of basic medical services, and low-cost housing has been socialized to a very limited extent by public financing. However, substitution of socialism for the present economic system in the United States and other capitalist countries is not generally believed to offer the ideal solution of the problem of equitable distribution of the fruits of science. Assuming a socialist system in which political liberties were enhanced rather than diminished, as may be the case in the cooperative communes in Israel, many questions as to incentives and as to who gets what would remain to be answered.

What all societies need, according to Victor C. Ferkiss, professor of government, is a system of social accounting

---

[26] Henry W. Riecken, "Social Science and Contemporary Social Problems," *S.S.R.C. Items,* March 1969, p. 3.
[27] Program on Technology and Society, *Fourth Annual Report* (1968), p. 51.

that would make clear the total costs and benefits of alternative proposals. "Such accounting is no longer impossible, thanks to refinements in data collecting and computerization of results."[28] But in the case, for example, of a proposal to expand food production, how to submit relevant data to the computer and how to obtain a printout telling the best way of proceeding and the costs involved would present problems for which system analysts do not have a solution. Social inventiveness will be needed to produce such solutions.

CREATION OF NEW PROBLEMS BY SOLUTION OF OLD

On what is attainable, Mesthene has written: "We now have, or know how to acquire, the technical capacity to do very nearly anything we want. Can we transplant human hearts, control personality, order the weather that suits us, travel to Mars or to Venus? Of course we can, if not now or in five or ten years, then certainly in twenty-five, or in fifty or a hundred."[29] Each scientific miracle, however, not only solves an old problem but presents new ones. This holds true in improvement of health, easing of toil, provision of goods and services, and other aspects of life.

The annual death rate per thousand, in England, dropped from about 36 in 1750 to 21 in 1821 and to 11 or 12 in the 1960s as a consequence of scientific advances. Life expectancy in the developed countries has doubled in the past 200 years, from 34 to 68 years. Further prolongation of life by means of scientific discoveries may reasonably be predicted,[30] but with the concomitant problem of what to do with the added years. H. Bentley Glass, academic vice president of the State University of New York at Stony Brook, has warned of the need to understand the problems which will emerge in genetics: "We are in the position of being the creators of the future living world. I do not believe we can continue to stand in that position blindly."[31]

Some scenarios of life as modified in future eras by science and technology have been based on the probability that resultant problems will be solved constructively. Edward

---

[28] Victor C. Ferkiss (Georgetown University), *Technological Man: The Myth and the Reality* (1969), p. 260.

[29] Emmanuel G. Mesthene, "Learning to Live With Science," *Saturday Review*, July 17, 1965, p. 14.

[30] See "Prolongation of Life," *E.R.R.*, 1966 Vol. II, pp. 513-515.

[31] Remarks at Twelfth International Congress on Genetics, Tokyo, Aug. 21, 1968. See also "Genetics and the Life Process," *E.R.R.*, 1967 Vol. II, pp. 920-922.

Science and Society

Bellamy, in *Looking Backward, 2000-1887* (1888), envisaged new, beneficial social structures. Jules Verne's stories of submarines and space flights presupposed the victory of good over evil. A vision of mental evolution in the direction of compassion toward one's fellow man was presented in the writings of Pierre Teilhard de Chardin. For the near future, scientists predict development, among other things, of a robot for housework, facsimile printing of news in the home, ocean farming,[32] and inexpensive desalination of water.

The possibility that the problems arising from increased ingenuity will overwhelm mankind, as predicted by Henry Adams, was dramatically exhibited in some of the novels of H. G. Wells. In more explicit terms, Oswald Spengler foretold the decline of western civilization as a natural aging process which must tear down even the most sophisticated intellectual edifices. Bertrand Russell, replying to J. B. S. Haldane's confident prediction of a millennium produced by science, wrote: "Much as I should like to agree with his forecast, . . . I am compelled to fear that science will be used to promote the power of dominant groups, rather than to make men happy."[33] Aldous Huxley's *Brave New World* and George Orwell's *Nineteen Eighty-four* were fictional exemplifications of what Russell feared.

SCIENCE AND WISDOM AS AIDS TO HUMAN HAPPINESS

A conscious effort will be needed to prevent perversion of the findings of science and to superintend the use of those findings in the interest of fulfillment rather than enslavement. Such an effort must be grounded in an enlightened view of the aspirations as well as the potentialities of man. Jacques Barzun, provost of Columbia University, discussing the relations of science and enlightenment, wrote:

> Unlike the oppressive creeds of the past, science is not to be fought by enlightenment. . . . It *is* enlightenment. . . . But there is around it an institution to understand and to control. If we postpone the task or fumble it, we may wake up to find that the pressures accumulating within mankind under its present unendurable strains will explode into a chaos where, for a longer or a shorter time, neither science nor social order will find a place.[34]

Success in steering the uses of science to achievement of worthy goals depends on a social consciousness which,

---

[32] See "Oceans and Man," *E.R.R.*, 1968 Vol. I, pp. 329-331.

[33] Bertrand Russell, *Icarus, or the Future of Science* (1924), p. 5, replying to Haldane's *Daedalus—or Science and the Future* (1923).

[34] Jacques Barzun, "Science as a Social Institution," in *Science and Human Affairs* (proceedings of the Academy of Political Science, New York, April 1966), p. 14.

according to A. Cornelius Benjamin, science itself cannot provide. Benjamin wrote: "The world will be neither saved nor destroyed, barring accidents, by science alone. It will be saved by men of knowledge and vision who use science to promote the good life; it will be destroyed by men of ignorance and myopia who use science to promote the bad life." [35]

Science needs to be supplemented by wisdom and good will not only to save the world but also to promote the happiness of individuals. Happiness for an individual is found, as Aristotle noted, in doing the best he can with the talents he has. Science can contribute most effectively to such self-fulfillment by facilitating satisfaction of primary needs and by providing man with a footing in his laborious climb toward understanding of himself, empathy with his fellow men, and exercise of creativity.

---

[35] A. Cornelius Benjamin (professor of philosophy, University of Missouri), *Science, Technology, and Human Values* (1965), p. 285.

WASTE DISPOSAL: COMING CRISIS

by

Richard L. Worsnop

1 9 6 9
Mar. 12

WASTE DISPOSAL: COMING CRISIS

A MERICA the beautiful is also America the wasteful, and as waste products accumulate, the beauty is apt to fade. Refuse litters the shore of San Francisco Bay. Liquid, solid and thermal effluents pour freely into Ohio rivers. The fumes of burning refuse darken the atmosphere of New York City. Discarded bottles, cans and paper deface highways and parks. The quality of American life—and life itself—is diminished.

Around $3 billion a year is spent in the United States on urban waste disposal, and that sum is not nearly enough. But additional money is not the only requirement. More ingenuity in disposing of waste materials is needed, as well as increased public awareness of the dimensions of the waste problem. Much of what is routinely thrown away is salvageable. The carcasses of old automobiles can be and to some extent are reclaimed as scrap metal; some waste paper is repulped; some manure is used as fertilizer. Most of these materials, however, become eyesores or pollutants, or both. Salvage of waste is expensive, but the economic and social costs of letting waste pile up at present rates promise to be infinitely greater.

CHANGES IN QUANTITIES AND VARIETIES OF REFUSE

Only a country as wealthy as the United States could afford to be wasteful on such a prodigious scale. In poorer lands, less is thrown away because there is less to throw away. Housewives carry groceries in reusable cloth or nylon-net shopping bags, not disposable paper bags; automobiles are driven, by those fortunate enough to own them, for many more years than in this country; newspapers often serve as wrapping paper or toilet tissue before being finally discarded. France, with its great variety of wines, has only a few types of wine bottles. "Except for Champagne and Alsace, all France gets along on two shapes, two colors, and one standard size. Bottles scarcely occur as litter in France. Even

45

those left by American tourists are soon picked up and re-circulated." [1]

In contrast, this country produces an awesome volume of rubbish. It is estimated that solid waste from the nation's urban areas aggregates one billion pounds a day or 185 million tons a year. This constitutes around 800 million cubic yards of waste; if all gathered in one place, the waste would form a cube measuring one-half mile on each side; or a belt six feet high and three feet wide stretching for 20,000 miles. In addition, solid waste from the mining and processing of minerals amounts to approximately one billion tons a year. Farms produce a billion tons of manure a year and, in combination with food processing industries, 200 million tons of crop residue; a part of the totals in both of those cases is usable as fertilizer.

The urban waste includes 30 million tons of paper, 4 million tons of plastics, 28 billion metal cans, and 26 billion bottles and jars a year. Discarded waste of all kinds in the country as a whole—garbage, paper, grass clippings, old autos, dead dogs and cats, demolition materials, and the like—averages out to between six and eight pounds per person per day, or about double the amount discarded 40 years ago. The U. S. Public Health Service expects that per-capita waste production will double in weight again within the next 20 years. "Furthermore, the *volume* of household waste is increasing far more rapidly than the weight. This reflects not only the shift toward paper but also the trend toward thinner grades of paper that, pound for pound, take up far more space when crumpled as refuse." [2]

A large and rapidly growing proportion of household waste consists of packaging materials. In former times, most beverage containers were returnable glass bottles which were reused many times. Today, in contrast, most beverage containers—whether made of glass, metal, or plastic—are non-returnable. Of the 30 billion beverage containers produced in 1966, only eight of every hundred were returnable. It is estimated that in 1976, when around 63 billion beverage containers will be produced, only three of every hundred will be returnable.

Plastic packaging materials pose a special problem. For

[1] George R. Stewart, *Not So Rich As You Think* (1967), p. 128.

[2] Tom Alexander, "Where Will We Put All That Garbage?" *Fortune*, October 1967, p. 150.

all practical purposes, plastics are indestructible; they do not decompose by oxidation, like metal cans, nor do they break down by bacterial action. In addition, plastics cannot be compressed in a sanitary landfill like collapsible metal cans or breakable glass bottles.[3] Burning of plastic wastes may be hazardous; polyethylene, a carbon-hydrogen combination, burns clean to carbon dioxide and water vapor, but polyvinyl chloride produces hydrochloric acid fumes when burned.

DISPOSAL BY DUMPING, INCINERATION AND LANDFILL

The problem of waste disposal cannot be separated from that of pollution of the air, water, and land environment. "These three realms," the Senate Public Works Committee's Subcommittee on Air and Water Pollution was told last summer, "are inevitably linked in urban areas: pollution of the air from municipal refuse dumps and outmoded incinerators; pollution of surface waters from industrial dumps, mill tailings, floating debris, and with the runoff from uncontrolled garbage dumping and filling areas; pollution of ground waters by infiltration of contaminated water from mineral dumps and refuse landfills; and desecration of the landscape by strip mines, tailings ponds and piles from the processing of coal and minerals." [4] Moreover, use of coastal areas or wetlands as garbage dumps destroys the breeding grounds of many species of birds and fish.[5]

There is nothing intrinsically wrong with burning or burying waste. The trouble is that it usually is burned improperly or buried in the wrong place.

Theoretically, high-temperature incinerators should be able to reduce the total volume of municipal wastes by 75 to 90 per cent, thereby cutting the demand for landfill. But almost none of the incinerators currently in operation in the U. S. meet the standards for air pollution emissions that most experts recommend. Some have been shut down for this reason. New incinerators have been designed with elaborate electrostatic precipitators and gas scrubbers that can meet these standards, but both capital and operating costs are extremely high—totaling five or six times as much as the cost of sanitary landfill. Furthermore, such incinerators are usually designed for more or less specific refuse components, and such specifics are hard to predict over the next decades. Paper dresses, for example,

[3] Charles A. Schweighauser of the Williams College Center for Environmental Studies reported, Feb. 11, 1969, on research in Sweden on a technique, involving sunlight and soil acids, to reduce bottles to powder; and research at Clemson University in South Carolina on means of dissolving bottles in water.

[4] Rolf Eliassen, professor of environmental engineering, Stanford University, July 9, 1968.

[5] See "Wildlife Preservation," *E.R.R.*, 1967 Vol. I, pp. 341-360.

are purposely made nonflammable, so that it takes higher-temperature incinerators to make them burn.[6]

Sanitary landfill is defined by the American Society of Civil Engineers as "a method of disposing of refuse on land without creating nuisances or hazards to public health or safety, by utilizing the principles of engineering to confine the refuse to the smallest possible area, to reduce it to the smallest practical volume, and to cover it with a layer of earth at the conclusion of each day's operation, or at such more frequent intervals as may be necessary." In calculating the amount of land needed for sanitary landfill for a given community, around 7 acre-feet (11,293) cubic yards per 10,000 persons per year is a frequently used rule of thumb.

Although landfill is a less expensive disposal method than incineration, appropriate sites sometimes are difficult to find. Size, proximity and accessibility are important factors, but geological considerations are, or should be, controlling. Only about 20 per cent of all municipal waste in the Washington, D. C., metropolitan area is buried in landfills. The reason is that many potential sites have thin soil cover or lie within the watersheds of public water supplies.

Probably the best sanitary-landfill system in the United States is in Los Angeles County, California. The system serves 70 separate municipalities, including a part of the city of Los Angeles itself. Extensive use of landfill has been imperative in the county since 1957, when municipal, industrial and private-home incinerators were ordered shut down to reduce smog.

The county was fortunate in having numerous natural canyons where refuse could be piled up to 600 feet deep. The various sanitation districts in the county banded together to buy an abandoned quarry at Palos Verdes for sanitary-landfill purposes. Residents of the area objected on the ground that the landfill would be unsightly and would exude smoke and odors. The sanitation districts promised that each day's load of refuse would be covered over and that the completed landfill would be a community asset. Within five years a section of the quarry had been converted into a public arboretum.

Land adjoining sanitary landfills now constitutes some of the choicest residential property in Los Angeles County.

---

[6] Tom Alexander, *op. cit.*, p. 151.

Waste Disposal: Coming Crisis

When the Mission Canyon Landfill was begun, nearby ridges were left in the hands of private subdividers. Their land was then split into one-third-acre parcels, each of which sold for $35,000 or more; the houses built on the lots were in the $70,000-$125,000 class. The completed landfill is destined to become a golf course that will provide surrounding homeowners with both recreation and a pleasant view. Landfilling in Los Angeles County also affords protection against landslides such as those which occurred during torrential rains in January and February 1969.

PROBLEM OF ANIMAL WASTE DISPOSAL ON FARMS

The waste-disposal problems of urban areas get most of the attention, but farming and forest regions produce a far greater volume of refuse. Domestic animals produce more than one billion tons of fecal wastes and 400 million tons of liquid wastes a year. If used bedding, paunch manure from abattoirs, and carcasses are included, the total annual production of animal wastes comes close to two billion tons. This is equivalent to the waste production of a human population of 1.9 billion.

Animal wastes formerly were considered a valuable agricultural asset. The 1938 *Yearbook of Agriculture,* for example, stated that "One billion tons of manure, the annual product of livestock on American farms, is capable of producing $3 billion worth of increase in crops."

> The potential value of this agricultural resource is three times that of the nation's wheat crop and equivalent to $440 for each of the country's 6,800,000 farm operators. The crop nutrients it contains would cost more than six times as much as was expended for commercial fertilizers in 1936. Its organic matter content is double the amount of soil humus annually destroyed in growing the nation's grain and cotton crops.

Today's farmer would much prefer to enrich his land with chemical fertilizers instead of manure. As a result, unwanted animal wastes accumulate in offensive-smelling piles or overloaded lagoons. Moreover, manure provides a spawning ground for vermin; on drying, it is a source of unsavory dusts; in rainstorms, it produces runoff water that absorbs large amounts of biochemical oxygen; and it may be the source of certain infectious agents found in streams.

The animal waste problem is particularly acute on livestock feedlots or poultry "factories," where several thousand animals or several hundred thousand birds are concentrated

49

in a small area. "For example, a feedlot carrying 10,000 head of cattle has about the same sewage disposal problem as a city of 164,000 people. The city will be using 8,200,000 gallons of water a day to carry off the sewage. Such amounts of water are never used and are seldom even available at the feedlot." [7]

The country's forests are plagued by logging debris, which accumulates at the rate of 25 million tons a year. Such debris serves as a breeding ground for tree disease organisms and insects, and it poses a serious fire hazard. The average size of forest fires originating in logging waste is more than seven times that of fires originating in uncut areas where trash has not accumulated. The only feasible way to dispose of logging debris is by burning, which contributes to pollution of the atmosphere.

Processing of farm and forest products results in additional waste-disposal problems. This kind of waste, usually dumped raw into rivers or streams, includes runoff or effluent from sawmilling; pulp, paper and fiberboard manufacturing; fruit and vegetable canning; cleaning of dairies; slaughtering and processing of meat animals; tanning; manufacturing of cornstarch and soy protein; sugar refining; malting, fermenting, and distilling; scouring of wool; and wet processing in textile mills. On entering a stream, these wastes greatly increase the consumption of oxygen. They may make the water unsightly, unpalatable, and malodorous.

The oxidative requirements of the effluent from the wood-pulp, paper and paperboard industries exceed those of the raw sewage from all the people of the United States. In a year's time, the canning industry produces effluent with oxidative demands that are double those of the raw sewage from metropolitan Detroit; the meat-packing industry, double those of metropolitan Chicago; and the dairy industry, four times those of metropolitan Boston.

DIFFICULTY IN GETTING RID OF NUCLEAR EFFLUENTS

A conspicuous exception to the careless disposal of waste in the United States is that of nuclear effluents. The total amounts of nuclear waste produced in this country in a year can be measured in pounds rather than tons. Nevertheless,

---

[7] U.S. Department of Agriculture, *Wastes in Relation to Agriculture and Forestry* (1968), p. 41.

apprehension over radioactive contamination is so great that extraordinary measures are taken to minimize the threat. Nuclear power plants create small amounts of gaseous waste. Dr. Glenn T. Seaborg, chairman of the U. S. Atomic Energy Commission, has said that "These gases, most of them inert and having a short half-life of radioactivity, are usually contained in the plant—sometimes as long as 30 days —and then after passing through high efficiency filters, to remove 99.9 per cent of air particulate matter, are discharged under favorable atmospheric conditions." More dangerous wastes, Seaborg says, are reduced "into a powder, a granular form or a glass-like substance" and deposited in worked-out salt mines.[8] Those like cesium-137 and strontium-90, which have an unusually long radioactive life, are placed in steel-lined concrete tanks and buried deep in the earth or sunk to the bottom of the sea.

Disposing of highly dangerous wastes in what seems like a safe manner can have unforeseen consequences. For example, the U. S. Army began in March 1962 to pump chemical wastes from the Rocky Mountain Arsenal near Denver into a 12,000-foot artificial well near the Colorado capital. A month later, Denver experienced its first earthquake in 80 years. In the next three and one-half years, 709 additional minor earthquakes shook Denver.

> The geologists, naturally, became interested. After a year or so, one of them was able to make a simple coordination. Soon after the time when effluent was poured into the deep hole, he discovered, there were earthquakes. When nothing was being poured in, the earthquakes soon stopped. The tremendous pressure exerted by such a high column of liquid, even if the liquid itself was not of great quantity, was enough to disturb the balance of the rocks.[9]

The arsenal's waste-disposal program now has been completely revamped; no chemical effluents are poured into the well. Dr. David M. Evans, of the Colorado School of Mines, told a symposium on environmental hazards in December 1968 that "If the authorities had decided to eliminate the contamination at its source to begin with, U. S. taxpayers would have been saved millions of dollars for damages to crops and real estate by contamination, another $1.5 million for the cost of the disposal well—and Denver would still be an earthquake-free city." [10]

---

[8] Testimony before Senate Public Works Subcommittee on air and water pollution, June 3, 1968.

[9] George R. Stewart, *op. cit.*, p. 71.

[10] Remarks at symposium on "Unanticipated Environmental Hazards Resulting From Technological Intrusions," Dallas, Texas, Dec. 28, 1968.

Evans also discounted the arguments of those who give the widespread use of oil field brine injection wells as a rationale for promoting underground waste injection. Citing specific examples of brine from such wells affecting surface waters, Evans further argued that waste wells have a greater chance of leaking than salt water wells. Oil field brine usually is injected into oil- and gas-depleted reservoirs, whereas industrial disposal wells discharge into zones already filled with salt water and raise the reservoir pressure above normal. "It may take decades, or even centuries, but this high pressure eventually will leak out," he said, "perhaps into other underground zones, perhaps to the surface, perhaps into public waters."

SERIOUS EFFECTS OF NEW YORK SANITATION STRIKE

If the Denver earthquakes illustrated the dangers in disposal of highly dangerous wastes, New York City's nine-day sanitation workers' strike in February 1968 vividly demonstrated the need for daily collection of ordinary municipal garbage and trash. Around 100,000 tons of uncollected refuse piled up in the city's streets before the dispute was settled. Mayor John V. Lindsay declared a citywide "health emergency" on the sixth day of the strike. The emergency would have been far more serious if the strike had occurred in the summer rather than during unseasonably cold winter weather.

The New York sanitation workers' strike had the additional effect of pointing up the high cost of waste disposal in a large city. Even before the walkout began, it was estimated that "It costs nearly $30 a ton to collect, transport, and dispose of New York's refuse—or three times the cost of a ton of West Virginia coal, mined and delivered in New York." [11] Around 75-85 per cent of that sum represents labor and transportation costs. Depositing waste in sanitary landfills normally costs between 70 cents and $2 a ton, while incineration costs between $4 and $6 a ton. It is estimated that about 40,000 vehicles in the United States are used exclusively for collection of solid wastes. These vehicles represent an investment value of about $400 million. Refuse collection trucks, varying in capacity from 10 to 30 cubic yards, cost anywhere from $10,000 to $30,000 per unit. In

---

[11] Tom Alexander, *op. cit.*, pp. 150-151.

addition, storage and maintenance facilities amount to about 12 per cent of the value of the mobile equipment.

In the country as a whole, municipalities and citizens pay $3 billion a year for waste disposal. The expenditure of local funds for solid waste is exceeded only by expenditures for schools and roads. Additional money and better disposal facilities are needed, but they may be difficult to obtain. Royce Hanson, president of the Washington Center for Metropolitan Studies, has explained why: "Unfortunately for solid waste, its management costs more than a street-crossing light or another policeman, but not as much as a power plant or a major dam. Waste management falls within that range of public expenditures which is too large to be considered trivial and yet not large enough to be beyond the comprehension of the average householder. There is also something ridiculous about a society spending more to rid itself of its wastes than to feed its poor." [12]

Early Methods of Disposing of Refuse

IF THE HISTORY of waste disposal could be plotted on graph paper, it would appear as a jagged line representing painfully slow advances and unaccountably sharp declines. In general, waste-disposal methods have been no better than they had to be, and they often have failed to meet even that modest standard. The author of a book on the waste problem theorizes that carelessness in disposing of refuse is a heritage of the time, millions of years ago, when man's ancestors lived in trees.

> The trees offered a built-in sanitation and refuse system. Whatever was discarded, it all fell neatly to the ground—excreta, nutshells, pods, hair-droppings. If, in these primitive years, there was such a phenomenon as a natural death, the dead body too, as its hands released hold, slumped off, fell, and disappeared. On the ground below, the humble scavengers and the processes of decay soon dissipated all such materials and returned them to the soil.[13]

Some ancient peoples were more adept at handling waste than others. The cities of Mesopotamia and the Indus

---

[12] Remarks before Surgeon General's Conference on Solid Waste Management for Metropolitan Washington, Washington, D.C., July 19, 1967.

[13] George R. Stewart, *op. cit.*, p. 9.

Valley, which flourished in the third millennium B.C., had elaborate systems of sewers and drains. On the other hand, excavations at the site of Troy indicate that the inhabitants dropped their refuse on the floor and let it accumulate. When the level rose so high that doors would not open, the doors were repositioned. Residents of ancient Athens deposited refuse in dumps at the borders of the city; unwanted babies also were left there to die.

MANNER OF DISCARDING REFUSE IN ANCIENT ROME

Lewis Mumford writes that ancient Rome, despite its engineering genius, reached "a low point in sanitation and hygiene that more primitive communities never descended to." It was the Roman practice to dispose of carcasses—both human and animal—in huge open pits on the outskirts of the city. The gladiatorial spectacles alone provided ample material for disposal. "As many as 5,000 animals, including creatures as large as the elephant and the water buffalo, might be slaughtered in a single day, to say nothing of the hundreds of human beings who were likewise done to death in the arena." [14]

Rodolfo Amadeo Lanciani, a noted Italian archaeologist, uncovered some of these pits in the 19th century. "It is hard," Lanciani wrote, "to conceive the idea of a Roman carnarium, an assemblage of pits into which men and beasts, bodies and carcasses, and any kind of unmentionable refuse, were thrown in disorder. Imagine what must have been the conditions of these dreadful districts in times of plague, when the pits . . . were kept open by night and day. And when the pits became filled, up to the mouth, the moat which skirted the walls of Servius Tullius, between the Colline and the Esquiline gates, was filled with corpses, thrown in as if they were carrion, until the level of the adjacent streets was reached."

Lanciani found about 75 pits, 12 feet square and 30 feet deep, filled with a "uniform mass of black, viscid, unctuous matter." On the day he found the third pit, Lanciani was "obliged to relieve [his] gang of workmen from time to time, because the stench from that putrid mound, turned up after a lapse of 20 centuries, was unbearable, even for men inured to every kind of hardship, as were my excavators." Waste disposal methods in medieval Europe were crude,

---

[14] Lewis Mumford, *The City in History* (1961), p. 217.

but evidence exists that governments and people of the time were aware of the problem. As early as 1388, the English Parliament passed an act that forbade throwing of filth and garbage into ditches, rivers, and waters. The poet John Lydgate, in his *Troy Book* (1412-20), went further; he proposed a system of conduit pipes with running water to carry off filth and ordure. The town employing such a system would, Lydgate wrote, be "utterly assured/From engendyring of all corrupcioun,/From wicked air and from infeccioun,/That causen ofte by her violence/Mortalitie and great pestilence."

The author of a *Survey of London* printed in 1528 mentioned a city ordinance which stated that "no man shall bury any dung or goung within the liberties of the city" nor "carry any ordure till after nine o'clock in the night"—in other words, after bedtime. The first public sewage plant is believed to have operated in the Silesian city of Bunzlau in 1543. The custom of lighting bonfires on summer festival days was perceived to have "the virtue that a great fire hath to purge the infection of the air."

Pigs were employed as scavengers in medieval towns. Mumford notes that "Non-edible waste was doubtless harder to dispose of: ashes, tannery offal, big bones; but certainly there was far less of this than in the modern city; for tins, iron, broken glass, bottles, and paper were scarce, or even non-existent." [15] In general, medieval refuse consisted of organic matter which decomposed and mingled with the earth.

DEPLORABLE SANITARY CONDITIONS IN 19TH CENTURY

Sanitary conditions in European towns and cities took a turn for the worse toward the close of the Middle Ages. The change was due to the introduction of multi-story tenement dwellings, often four or five floors high. People living on the upper floors would throw waste out their windows onto the street below rather than carry it downstairs.

The waste problem reached staggering proportions in the early years of the industrial revolution. Hugh Miller, writing of Manchester in 1862, noted that "Nothing seems more characteristic of the great manufacturing city, though disagreeably so, than the river Irwell, which runs through the place." The author explained: "There are myriads of dirty

---

[15] *Ibid.*, pp. 292-293.

things given it to wash, and whole wagonloads of poisons from dye houses and bleachyards thrown into it to carry away; steam boilers discharge into it their seething contents, and drains and sewers their fetid impurities; till at length it rolls on—here between tall dingy walls, there under precipices of red sand-stone—considerably less a river than a flood of liquid manure."

Poorly ventilated workers' houses were built back-to-back near factories, sometimes on land filled in with ashes and broken glass and rubbish. Waste collection was virtually non-existent; hence the inhabitants of these industrial slums would throw their refuse into the streets. It would remain there "until the accumulation induced someone to carry it away for manure." Open drains represented comparatively advanced waste disposal, despite their stench and the health hazard they posed.

Improvements finally came toward the end of the 19th century. Even in an age of laissez faire capitalism, it was obvious that private companies were unequal to the task of maintaining a tolerable level of sanitation. Thus, what Sidney and Beatrice Webb called "municipal socialism" came into being. Such essential community-wide services as water supply and sewage systems developed as collectively owned and operated utilities. By 1900, the standard of one private, sanitary toilet per family had been firmly established.

Proposals to Improve Waste Disposal

THE SANITARY IMPROVEMENTS of the late 19th century have been extended, but they have not been altered to meet changing conditions. The great increase of population density in urban areas and the consequent rise in waste volume have created problems that present disposal methods are ill-equipped to handle. As a result, local governments and the federal government are belatedly searching for new approaches and new technology to deal with the waste crisis.

ADVANTAGES IN REGIONAL APPROACH TO THE PROBLEM

A major obstacle to improvement of present waste disposal methods is political in nature. The urban waste problem, like the related environmental pollution problem, is a regional one; yet both problems are attacked primarily on the local level. Individual municipalities often lack the financial resources to dispose of their waste satisfactorily. At the same time, they have shown little interest in pooling resources with neighboring communities to better meet a common problem.

A report prepared two years ago for former Secretary of Health, Education and Welfare John W. Gardner emphasized the need for regional solutions to urban waste problems.

> There must be an inducement so strong for state and local governments to do comprehensive planning on an appropriate geographic scale and to conform with national goals and objectives that it is politically and economically unpalatable for them to do otherwise. . . . Participation on the part of local government in any regional environmental program should be as great as possible, but it must be recognized that environmental protection problems will have to be solved on the metropolitan or regional scale. We must engage in experimentation and research in order to increase our capacity to make decisions at the metropolitan or regional level.[16]

The experience of Los Angeles County provides an illustration of the advantages of an areawide approach to waste disposal. As noted, 70 separate communities in the county are served by a common waste disposal system. Collection and disposal costs—even with high land prices and long hauls to landfill sites—are among the lowest in the country. In the City of Los Angeles, they average $12 a ton, or almost one-third of the cost in New York. The Los Angeles County Sanitation Districts thus can afford a staff of engineers to research various advanced schemes for waste transportation and disposal—schemes which might be adopted after available landfill sites have been exhausted about 50 years from now.

The Washington, D. C., area waste disposal program may be uniquely difficult. Washington itself is a federal enclave whose suburbs lie in two different states—Maryland and Virginia. For this reason, it has been suggested that an interstate compact agency be created to deal with the national capital area's waste and related problems. A participant in the Surgeon General's Conference on Solid Waste Management for Metropolitan Washington in 1967 suggested that any areawide waste-disposal program "must be concerned

---

[16] The Task Force on Environmental Health and Related Problems, *A Strategy for a Livable Environment; a Report to the Secretary of Health, Education and Welfare* (1967), p. 1.

not only with solid waste disposal problems but air quality, water pollution, water quality and supply, chemical and pesticide hazard control and all other threats to our environment and our physical well being."

FEDERAL LAWS TO PROMOTE BETTER WASTE CONTROL

Passage of the Solid Waste Disposal Act of 1965 enabled localities and states to look to the federal government for help in solving waste problems. The law authorizes action in six areas of need: (1) Grants for local and state projects to demonstrate new and improved waste-disposal technology; (2) grants for the development of areawide solid waste management systems to end fragmentation of responsibilities among small communities; (3) grants for state surveys of solid waste handling needs and development of statewide plans for meeting these needs; (4) research, both direct and grant-supported, to establish the basis for new approaches to solid waste handling; (5) training programs, both direct and grant-supported, to alleviate critical shortages of trained personnel; and (6) technical assistance to local and state governments with solid waste problems.

The Solid Waste Disposal Act directs the Secretary of the Interior to help solve solid waste problems resulting from extracting, processing or using minerals or fossil fuels. All other responsibilities under the act are assigned to the Secretary of Health, Education and Welfare. On Dec. 3, 1965, the U. S. Surgeon General established the Solid Wastes Program of the National Center for Urban and Industrial Health to carry out the H.E.W. provisions of the act.

Projects that have received grants under the 1965 act to demonstrate new and improved disposal technology are oriented also toward finding constructive uses for waste materials. The use of wastes in reclaiming worthless land is the objective of a number of federally supported projects. Others seek to (1) reduce food wastes through development of spoilage-resistant fruits and vegetables; (2) convert wastes from citrus-fruit processing into citric acids; (3) transform cottage cheese and tomato wastes into human and animal foods.

Training of persons qualified to deal with solid waste problems is one of the most important undertakings of the 1965 act. In the past, few graduate school candidates in the environmental health field had elected to do graduate work in the solid waste field because of the tendency of the engineering profession and of public officials to give solid waste programs low priority. But now federal grants for solid waste training have been made to the University of Florida, Georgia Tech, the University of Michigan, Rensselaer Polytechnic Institute, the University of Texas, and other institutions.

SALVAGING OF WASTE MATERIALS FOR VARIOUS USES

Much of today's waste has some salvage value. The trouble is that the cost of processing, say, automobile carcasses to obtain steel usually is greater than that of using freshly mined iron ore. This being the case, Dr. Athelstan Spilhaus, who served as chairman of a waste-management committee of the National Academy of Sciences–National Research Council, has suggested that junked autos be piled into landscaped hills that could be mined when some future shortage of high-grade iron ore made scrap more valuable.

It sometimes happens that material once regarded as waste turns out to possess great value. Cotton wastes provide a striking example. Before invention of the cotton gin, the seeds from hand-separated cotton bolls were left to rot on or near the farms where the cotton was grown. But the large quantities of seed that accumulated at the gins could not be disposed of so easily. In the long run, four different uses were found for the seeds.

The short cotton lint—cotton linters—left on the seeds was used in production of smokeless powder and celluloid, and to impart greater tearing strength to certain grades of paper. After removal of the cotton linters, the cottonseed was separated into hull and meat. The hulls could be included as roughage in cattle feed, employed as a filler in different kinds of padding, and added to fertilizers as a diluent. The meats were pressed to yield a valuable oil that could be subjected to a steaming process to produce an edible oil or combined with hydrogen to produce a solid edible fat resembling lard. The cake left after removal of the oil was found to contain a high percentage of protein valuable as an organic source of nitrogen in fertilizers or as a vital compound in certain cattle feeds. "So successful was this industry built upon recovery of these wastes that cotton growers sought bald cotton . . . to grow primarily for these by-products when the rise of synthetic fibers (especially rayon) cut into the market for lint cotton." [17]

Some uses have been found for even the waste produced by pulp mills. It is employed in road surfacing, as a foaming agent, as a binder and adhesive, as a raw material for the synthesis of vanillin, and as the culture medium for growth of a type of yeast that can be fed to farm animals. However, the foregoing uses of pulp waste account for only a tiny fraction of the total volume of waste material.

Use of solid urban waste as a soil nutrient is frequently proposed. Chicago already helps to defray the high cost of disposing of the semi-solid, nutrient-rich "sludge" residue from its sewage treatment plants by drying it and shipping it to Florida for use on citrus groves. Now the Sanitary District of Greater Chicago is considering a method for disinfecting sewage sludge with nuclear radiation. The process would both sterilize and deodorize the sludge, enabling it to be piped to open country and dumped on ground which might later be used for farming. A proposed $6 million irradiation plant could process about two million gallons of sludge a day, or about 20 per cent of the daily total handled by the city's sanitary district.

European methods of recovering compost material from waste appear more advanced than those in the United States. A study team of the U.S. Solid Wastes Program, visiting West Germany in 1967, reported on the operation of a sewage treatment plant at Duisburg. Refuse brought to the plant is first picked over for salvageable bottles, cans, rags, cardboard, and so forth. Sewage sludge then is added to the remainder, and the mixture is put into a rotating drum for three to five days. The resulting compost is sieved and piled outside to cure, after which it is sold to landscape architects for use in new gardens.

In isolated West Berlin, the study group found, waste has still another use. Incinerator residue is run over a magnet to remove cans and metal, then crushed and sieved. The sieved material is mixed with charcoal and recycled cinder material and passed through a sintering oven. The end product, after resieving, is a lightweight aggregate material used for concrete block construction and for roadbed sub-base. "It must be pointed out," the study group stated, "that the situation

---

[17] David H. Killeffer, "Packing Pollution," *Saturday Review*, March 2, 1968, p. 56.

in West Berlin is very special; regular gravel and aggregate must be shipped in across the 110 miles of East Germany, and not only is there the shipping cost, but East Germany collects a toll on its passage." Nevertheless, the West Berlin experience suggests that many constructive uses for waste can be found when raw materials are not readily available.

DISPOSAL OF REFUSE BY LONG-HAUL RAIL TRANSPORT

Almost all municipal waste at present is burned, buried or otherwise disposed of close to the point of origin. But several cities are considering ways to dispose of refuse in remote areas served by railroads. Philadelphia, for example, wants to initiate a rail-haul program under which municipal waste would be transported to northeastern Pennsylvania and used as cover for worked-out strip mines. David Smallwood, the city streets commissioner, said on March 2 that if the state withholds approval of the plan Philadelphia may be forced to dispose of some of its refuse in the Atlantic Ocean.

San Francisco, hemmed in on three sides by water, is trying to work out an arrangement for depositing its refuse in sanitary landfills in sparsely inhabited Lassen County, 375 miles to the north of the city. The projected landfill site consists of desert terrain unsuited at present for either grazing or agriculture. The nutrients added to the soil by the covered-over waste might eventually make the land arable. In the meantime, the City of San Francisco would pay Lassen County around $500,000 a year for waste-disposal rights. The alternative to long-haul waste disposal would be continued use of the shore of San Francisco Bay as a dumping ground. The area of the bay already has shrunk by one-third in the past century because of garbage dumping and other landfilling activity, and conservationists are determined to prevent further intrusions.

STREET CRIME IN AMERICA

by

Hoyt Gimlin

**1 9 6 9
Jan. 22**

STREET CRIME IN AMERICA

S TREET CRIME is the most visible and usually the most violent of the many varieties of crime in the United States. It instills fear in the citizenry and a new uncertainty in politics. Few of the country's domestic problems are as pervasive, as complex, or as difficult to solve. Government is nevertheless expected to take effective action to remedy, or at least alleviate, the situation.

The Gallup polling organization reported toward the end of the 1968 presidential campaign that the "most emotionally charged" issue before the voters was that of crime and disorder in the cities and on college campuses. In this setting, all three leading presidential candidates spoke out strongly for maintenance of law and order. The Republican platform voiced the party's determination "not to tolerate violence."

When Richard M. Nixon as President-elect introduced to a national television audience, Dec. 11, the men he had chosen to serve in his Cabinet, he described John N. Mitchell, the Attorney General-designate, as "a man who is as devoted as I am . . . to waging an effective war against crime in this country." Evelle J. Younger, Los Angeles district attorney who headed a Nixon task force on law and order, had already predicted that the new President would take a "no nonsense" approach to crime by seeking to broaden the use of wiretapping in law enforcement,[1] by appointing judges who would take a tough line on the rights of suspects, and by asking Congress to approve massive federal aid to local police.[2] When the task force submitted its final recommendations to Nixon on Jan. 11, Younger said: "We are not prepared to accept the proposition that the nation must continue to experience a crime wave."

---

[1] At a hearing before the Senate Judiciary Committee, Jan. 14, prior to his confirmation, the Attorney General-designate said that the Justice Department under the new regime would make use of authority granted by the Omnibus Crime Control and Safe Streets Act of (June 19) 1968 to employ wiretapping and other electronic devices "not only in national security cases but against organized crimes and other major crimes."

[2] Interview with *U. S. News & World Report*, Dec. 9, 1968, p. 78.

The Nixon administration's initial endeavors on the crime front may well benefit from the dominant view in Congress that the public is impatient with continuing violence in the streets and will welcome a "get tough" policy to curb crime. That view enabled Sen. John L. McClellan (D Ark.) and other leading conservatives of both parties in Congress to write into the Omnibus Crime Control and Safe Streets Act approved June 19, 1968, provisions calculated to undercut a series of Supreme Court decisions defining the rights of suspects during police investigations.

There has long been division over the best approach to crime control. President Johnson's Attorney General, Ramsey Clark, contended that crime, especially street crime, was caused at bottom by social and economic factors and could be eradicated in the long run only by means of anti-poverty and other remedial measures. Clark was a natural campaign target for Nixon, who accused him of "leading an official retreat" in the face of rising crime.

Whatever the differences over methods of attacking crime, President Johnson left no doubt of his abhorrence of the existing situation. In his valedictory State of the Union address, Jan. 14, he announced that he would propose in his budget message the next day that Congress appropriate for fiscal 1970 the full $300 million already authorized for aid to state and local law enforcement agencies. Johnson then went on to say: "I believe this is an essential contribution to justice and the public order in the United States. . . . But all this is only a small part of the total effort that must be made, . . . chiefly by the local governments throughout the nation, if we expect to reduce the toll of crime that we all detest."

DEFICIENCIES IN THE OFFICIAL STATISTICS ON CRIME

Americans know—or think—that there is an enormous amount of crime in this country. But even the experts do not pretend to know how much crime there is, because crime reporting is subject to glaring weaknesses. "Accurate data are the beginning of wisdom," the Wickersham Commission observed in 1931 in its report on criminal activity in the United States. Thirty-six years later, the President's Crime Commission [3] reported that its own surveys indicated that as

---

[3] Officially, the President's Commission on Law Enforcement and Administration of Justice. The 29-member commission, headed by Nicholas deB. Katzenbach, a former Attorney General, issued a 340-page report, *The Challenge of Crime in a Free Society*, in February 1967.

Street Crime in America

(per 100,000 population)

Area	Murder**	Forcible rape	Robbery	Aggravated assault
Anaheim-Santa Ana-Garden Grove, Calif.	1.7	16.3	56.9	81.4
Atlanta	13.3	15.3	60.5	92.0
Baltimore	11.3	27.6	353.0	378.3
Boston-Lowell-Lawrence, Mass.	3.2	7.7	66.8	68.7
Buffalo	2.8	15.8	83.5	76.9
Chicago	9.5	24.2	294.5	229.6
Cincinnati, Ohio-Ky.-Ind.	6.7	12.0	62.4	89.5
Cleveland	8.4	8.6	188.8	87.0
Dallas	11.1	14.0	79.6	205.9
Denver	4.0	28.2	105.4	109.5
Detroit	8.9	28.7	341.3	197.8
Houston	16.9	17.1	194.8	189.5
Indianapolis	6.6	22.3	131.7	61.4
Kansas City, Mo.-Kan.	8.0	25.1	214.2	165.3
Los Angeles-Long Beach	7.0	35.4	234.3	269.6
Miami	11.3	18.1	279.1	358.1
Milwaukee	3.6	5.4	54.9	51.7
Minneapolis-St. Paul	2.1	15.0	137.6	101.9
Newark, N. J.	6.1	13.9	152.6	157.8
New Orleans	14.2	29.7	222.4	236.3
New York City	7.0	17.6	317.5	224.1
Paterson-Clifton-Passaic, N. J.	2.2	5.0	47.3	67.6
Philadelphia, Pa.-N. J.	6.3	14.6	81.6	104.5
Pittsburgh	3.0	10.2	98.4	67.4
St. Louis, Mo.-Ill.	10.6	19.9	169.7	150.2
San Bernardino-Riverside-Ontario, Calif.	5.1	23.7	60.4	145.7
San Diego	3.2	14.2	51.0	74.8
San Francisco-Oakland	6.0	22.2	226.8	158.5
Seattle-Everett	4.9	17.1	99.9	93.1
Washington, D. C.	8.6	15.8	263.0	187.5

* Areas embrace one or more central cities of at least 50,000 population and the adjoining suburbs.
** Includes non-negligent manslaughter.
SOURCE: Adapted from Federal Bureau of Investigation *Uniform Crime Reports—1967*, pp. 80-93, source of latest available annual statistics.

---

many as one-half of the crimes in selected major cities went unreported. Victims of unreported crimes told commission interviewers they did not inform the police because they thought the police could do nothing for them.

The best, and almost the only, present statistical information on the volume of crime in the United States is provided by a reporting system that has been painstakingly developed

over the years by the Federal Bureau of Investigation. The
F.B.I. compiles Uniform Crime Reports annually from statistics supplied by about 8,000 police agencies, whose jurisdiction embraces about 92 per cent of the population. But
notwithstanding continuing efforts to improve the reporting
methods, criminologists still speak of "the vagaries of police
bookkeeping."

The President's Crime Commission cited instances of city
police departments withholding or altering crime statistics
in years past. Patrick V. Murphy, director of the Law Enforcement Assistance Administration created in the Department of Justice by the Crime Control and Safe Streets Act,
said that "When I was a rookie in the 72nd Precinct in
Brooklyn, no police commander worth his salt would admit
he couldn't control crime and he proved it by controlling
crime statistics." [4] James Q. Wilson, a leading criminologist,
wrote in 1966 that "What appears to be a crime explosion
may in fact be a population explosion." There are more serious and violent crimes every year, he said, "simply because
there are more young people every year, and because young
people have always had a higher crime rate than adults." [5]

Experts who are critical of crime statistics do not doubt
that there is an actual, though undetermined, increase in
crime rates. Profs. Marvin E. Wolfgang of the University of
Pennsylvania and Lloyd E. Ohlin of the Harvard Law School
were quoted by the *New York Times,* Aug. 27, 1968, as saying they had been led to this conclusion by robbery figures in
the 1967 Uniform Crime Reports. The reported increase in
robberies amounted to 27 per cent over the previous year.
Ohlin explained that robberies are usually committed against
strangers and thus are almost always reported.

Robbery is one of 28 crimes listed in the annual Uniform
Crime Reports, and one of seven which the F.B.I. includes in
an index of serious crime. The other "index crimes" are
murder, rape, aggravated assault, burglary, motor vehicle
theft, and other thefts involving amounts of $50 or more.
Some 3.8 million index crimes were reported to the F.B.I.
in 1967, 16 per cent more than during the previous year.
Among these were 500,000 crimes involving violence, also 16

---

[4] Quoted by David Burnham, *New York Times,* Jan. 2, 1969.

[5] James Q. Wilson, "Crime in the Streets," *Public Interest,* Fall 1966, p. 32. Wilson
is professor of government at Harvard and author of *Varieties of Police Behavior*
(1968).

per cent more than in 1966. F.B.I. statistics for the first nine months of 1968 showed that the same categories of crime were continuing to rise.

CHARACTERISTICS OF THE WAVE OF STREET CRIME

Urban crime rates tend to be highest in the inner city and to decrease as the distance from the inner city increases. The 56 largest American cities, those of more than 250,000 population, accounted for 71 per cent of all robberies reported to the F.B.I. in 1967. The President's Crime Commission calculated that, nationally, the chances of being physically attacked or threatened were about 1 in 550. But the same studies indicated that the risk to a slum dweller was considerably greater—and that the risk of being attacked by a relative or acquaintance was twice as great as that of being attacked by a stranger. A police study conducted in Chicago in late 1965 and early 1966 found that for a Negro man the risk was six times greater than for a white person, and for a Negro woman eight times greater.

The President's Commission on Crime in the District of Columbia reported that Negroes in Washington were the "primary victims of serious crimes, with the exception of robbery and commercial housebreaking." Between 1950 and 1965, according to the commission, 56 per cent of the robbery victims in Washington were white. But during the same period 78 per cent of all murder victims were black, as were over 80 per cent of all women who were raped. And between 1961 and 1965, of the girls under 16 who were raped, 91 per cent were Negro.

At the same time, the Negro is more likely to be a perpetrator of crime. Negroes accounted for only 13 per cent of the nation's population in 1967 but, according to F.B.I. compilations, for one-third of all the adults and one-fourth of all the juveniles arrested. However, there is abundant evidence that crime is not simply the handiwork of a small segment of Americans, black or white. One boy in six is in trouble with the law before he reaches his 18th birthday. The American law enforcement system handles about 1.3 million offenders daily, and in the average year about 2.5 million Americans go to jail or prison.

The total cost to the taxpayers of maintaining police, courts and penal institutions exceeds $4 billion a year. The hidden cost of crime runs to countless billions. Much of this cost stems from "white collar crime"—that of business executives conspiring to fix prices, loan sharks swindling their clients, or bank clerks embezzling bank funds. Street crime, in contrast, is likely to be that of a tough teen-ager snatching a woman's purse or mugging someone in the park.

Street crime is associated with two powerful social trends: the increased urbanization of America and the increasing size and restiveness of its youth population. As long as crime statistics have been compiled—since 1930 by the F.B.I.— they have shown that males between the ages of 15 and 24 years constitute the largest group of lawbreakers. Today almost one-half of all Americans are 25 or younger.[6]

EARLIER CRIME WAVES; PREVALENCE OF FEAR TODAY

Lack of consensus on the causes and cures of present-day crime may result from the fact that it has been studied and analyzed so little. As a consequence, trends are hard to identify or explain. Whether the United States is more law-abiding—or less—than in its earlier years is largely a matter of conjecture. Through a selective reading of history and literature a persuasive argument can be made for either case. Violence in American life has been recorded since colonial days[7]; "frontier justice" was synonymous with vigilante action and the lynch mob. Sen. Ralph W. Yarborough (D Texas), testifying before the Senate Judiciary Subcommittee on Criminal Laws and Procedures, July 12, 1967, said: "In my state . . . even when I was a small boy, many people carried pistols. They were supposed to protect themselves and their families. It was about the only law enforcement we had."

Vincent L. Broderick, a former police commissioner of New York City, told the subcommittee the same day: "I question whether the streets of most cities are less safe today than they were 30 years ago, or 50 years ago. New York City was wracked, little more than 100 years ago, by riots more devastating and more wanton than any this country has seen in recent years; fifty years and thirty years ago there were sections of New York through which no police officer would think of patrolling alone."

New York City was virtually given over to rioters protesting the Civil War draft in July 1863. Mobs wrecked draft

---

[6] See "Population Profile of the United States," *E.R.R.*, 1967 Vol. II, pp. 803-820.
[7] See "Violence in American Life," *E.R.R.*, 1968 Vol. I, pp. 407-423.

offices, invaded an arsenal, sacked the mayor's residence, and looted and burned many stores. Negroes were hunted down and beaten. Before order could be restored, several police stations had been abandoned to the mob and set afire.

In his account of growing up in Harlem in the 1930s and 1940s, Claude Brown related *(Manchild in the Promised Land)* that the young people who spent their lives on the streets made their own rules and lived by their own code. There was no other security for them—just as there was not on the Texas frontier in the time of Sen. Yarborough's forebears.

Sen. Robert C. Byrd (D W.Va.) told the Senate in October 1968, after a visit to Russia, that he and his wife felt safer on the streets of Moscow than in some areas of Washington. About the same time, Drew Pearson made a similar observation about the safety of streets in the Communist capitals of Warsaw and Budapest. Pearson commented that the price of such safety was life in a police state. Stephen S. Rosenfeld, a former Moscow correspondent for the *Washington Post,* tends to agree. He wrote in that newspaper, Nov. 19, 1968, that while living in Moscow he sometimes had "the sense of a policeman standing every hundred meters." However, in Western Europe, where police repression is slight or totally absent, all available evidence points to lower crime rates than in the United States.

Scotland Yard has reported that Greater London, with its 790 square miles and 10 million people, had 205 armed robberies in 1967, the last year for which statistics have been published. Paris, with a population of just under three million, had only 20 armed robberies in 1967. By way of contrast, Washington, D.C., alone had 2,429 armed robberies in 1967 and 4,640 in 1968. Washington's population is about 850,000 although the metropolitan area has 2.8 million residents.

But comparisons with other times and places have little significance for people who feel themselves endangered. The President's Crime Commission reported that one-third of those it had questioned across the nation said they were afraid to walk alone in their neighborhoods after dark. In high-crime areas of two large cities, 43 per cent of the respondents said they stayed off the streets altogether at night. James Q. Wilson has noted that "Even social scientists who

71

write articles demonstrating that the alleged 'crime wave' is a statistical illusion are likely to tell their wives (or even themselves) that . . . they should not walk the streets alone after dark." [8]

Problems of Criminal Justice System

THE AMERICAN SYSTEM of criminal justice is indicted almost daily either in Congress, in scholarly journals, or on ghetto street corners. The critics are as diverse as their criticism, but in common they profess a belief that one or another of the system's key elements fails to function properly. These elements are the courts, the police, and the correctional institutions. Their activities are attracting attention because crime, particularly street crime, is attracting attention.

Some of the most volatile social problems of the 1960s have been thrust upon the policeman. George Edwards, a former police commissioner (1961-63) of Detroit who is now a federal judge, wrote in the *Michigan Law Review* in November 1965: "Hostility between the Negro communities of our large cities and the police departments is the major problem of law enforcement in this decade." In a study of riot-control measures, Gerry Willis wrote three years later: "The anger vented on police is a stored-up frustration with the whole 'system.' The cop is thought of as the Establishment's hired gun, enforcing the whole network of injustice."[9]

The policeman is expected to enforce the law, but with compassion and full regard for the constitutional rights of individuals. The difficulty of striking that delicate balance is attested by the prevalence of cries of "police brutality" from one direction and of "soft on criminals" from another. Policemen are often frustrated by lack of authority to enforce the law as rigorously as they think it should be enforced. "Formerly, the police were charged with being indifferent to crime; now they are accused of being preoccupied with it. In the past, police morality was characterized as too loose; now it is branded as too puritanical. Cops who

---

[8] James Q. Wilson, *op. cit.*, p. 28.
[9] Gerry Wills, *The Second Civil War* (1968), p. 82.

once tolerated brothels are now chided for seizing erotic books. . . ." [10] Off-duty white policemen, some of them wearing Wallace campaign buttons, beat up members of the militant Black Panthers in the corridors of a Brooklyn courthouse last summer; in the fall, two policemen were dismissed from the force in Oakland, Calif., for shooting up the Black Panther headquarters there.

Police action against street protesters during the Democratic National Convention in Chicago was characterized as a "police riot" in a study for the National Commission on the Causes and Prevention of Violence issued Dec. 1, 1968. [11] The police were provoked by taunts, curses and obscenities shouted by Yippies and student anti-war demonstrators, but there was "no doubt that police discipline broke during the melee." Some of the demonstrators seemed determined to cause trouble, and some of the police to take vengeance. During the convention Mayor Richard J. Daley vigorously defended the police and said they were portrayed unfairly by the news media. These points were reiterated in a formal report issued by the City of Chicago on Sept. 6, 1968.

SUPREME COURT DECISIONS ON RIGHTS OF SUSPECTS

The policeman's job—as he sees it—has been made more difficult by the "permissiveness" of society in general and by the so-called Negro revolution in particular. And he is wont to believe that the courts are quicker to see the criminal's rights than his own. Three Supreme Court decisions— Mallory, Miranda and Wade—have been especially distressing to police officers. The decisions spell out various rights of suspects during police questioning. The first of these rulings came in 1957 when the Court in Mallory v. United States (354 U.S. 449) held that if there was unnecessary delay in bringing the suspect before a judge for arraignment, any confession he made during that period could not be admitted in court as evidence against him.

Sen. Strom Thurmond (R S.C.), among others in Congress, has attributed the increase of crime in the District of Columbia to the "Mallory rule." That rule has applied only to federal (including District of Columbia) law-enforcement

---

[10] James Q. Wilson, *New York* magazine, May 27, 1968, in review of *The Police Establishment*, by William G. Turner, an ex-F.B.I. agent.

[11] The 13-member commission, headed by Milton S. Eisenhower, was appointed by President Johnson on June 5, 1968, the day Sen. Robert F. Kennedy (D N.Y.) was mortally wounded by an assassin. The Chicago study was conducted by a staff under Daniel Walker, president of the unofficial Chicago Crime Commission.

agencies, but on Nov. 10, 1968, the Court heard oral arguments on whether it should be considered to extend also to state jurisdictions.

In the case of Miranda *v.* Arizona (384 U.S. 436), the Court said in 1966 that before the police conduct an interrogation, they must advise the suspect that anything he says may be used as evidence against him; that he has a right to remain silent; and that he is entitled to have a lawyer present during questioning. The following year, in United States *v.* Wade (388 U.S. 218), the Court held that a pre-trial lineup constitutes a critical step in a criminal prosecution and that a defendant is entitled to the assistance of counsel at that stage.

On the other hand, the Supreme Court on June 10, 1968, sustained by an 8-1 vote the right of policemen to "stop and frisk" suspicious-looking persons. The Court's opinion, delivered by Chief Justice Earl Warren, stressed the need to protect policemen in their efforts to control street crime. Warren laid down a rule that permits police officers to search suspects when "a reasonably prudent man in the circumstances would be warranted in the belief that his safety or that of others was in danger." The Court rejected the argument of civil liberty and civil rights groups that a New York "stop and frisk" law violated the Fourth Amendment, which protects "the right of the people to be secure in their persons, houses, papers and effects, against unreasonable searches and seizures. . . ."

Congressional Quarterly has noted a marked change of attitude toward criminal defendants on the part of the Supreme Court. It has pointed out that most of the Court's decisions in significant criminal cases during the 1966-67 term went against the defendant in favor of broader police and prosecution powers; [12] the Court sustained the right of police officers to search and seize evidence, to use eavesdropping equipment, and to avail themselves of the services of informants and undercover agents.

Because the Crime Control and Safe Streets Act of 1968 contains provisions to nullify restrictions and requirements imposed by the Mallory, Miranda and Wade decisions, the question in many legal minds now is whether the Supreme Court will declare unconstitutional the pertinent provisions

---

[12] *1967 CQ Almanac,* p. 1154.

of the 1968 act. Before he left office, Attorney General Clark instructed federal law enforcement agents not to invoke the new provisions, thus lessening the chance that a test case would be brought soon. The 1968 act provides that a confession is admissible as evidence if it is made voluntarily, even if the suspect has not been warned of his constitutional rights. It states also that the police may hold a suspect in custody for six hours before arraignment—or longer in some situations—and still obtain an admissible confession. It further provides for the admissibility of eyewitness testimony obtained by the identification of a suspect in a police lineup, even if the suspect is without a lawyer at the time.

DANGERS IN RELEASE OF ACCUSED PERSONS ON BAIL

Under the American system of criminal justice, an individual may be punished only if he has been proved guilty, in a deliberate and impartial process, of violating a specific law. Hence when a person is formally charged and arraigned before a magistrate, he moves from the jurisdiction of the police to the criminal court—"the institution around which the rest of the system of criminal justice has developed and to which the rest of the system is in large measure responsible." [13]

Typically, the heavy load of pending court cases prevents the magistrate from taking more than a cursory look at the case before he hears the defendant's plea. If the plea is guilty, the magistrate designates a date for sentencing; if the plea is not guilty, he fixes bail and sets a trial date, and perhaps appoints counsel if the defendant is indigent.

Bail is a device, borrowed from ancient England, making it practical to allow a defendant to remain free until he is tried. If he fails to appear for trial, the bail money posted in his behalf is forfeited. The Eighth Amendment declares that bail shall not be "excessive." A provision of law enacted by the First Congress in 1789, still in effect, states that in all except cases involving the death penalty the defendant "shall" be given an opportunity to post bail.

In practice, however, a defendant often stayed behind bars awaiting trial if the judge feared—or was persuaded by the prosecutor or police—that his release would be dangerous to society. Bail was simply set so high that the defendant could not raise it. This practice, while protecting

---

[13] President's Commission on Law Enforcement and Administration, *op. cit.*, p. 125.

the community, had the effect of keeping poor defendants in jail for months awaiting trial. Sometimes they were found innocent.

Bail reformers in New York, Chicago, St. Louis, Des Moines and Washington conducted experiments in the early 1960s on release of defendants without bail. They concluded that those with community and family ties were unlikely to run away. Partly on the basis of these findings, Congress enacted the Bail Reform Act of 1966, the first significant change in bail procedures since passage of the Judiciary Act of 1789. The 1966 law gave federal judges wide leeway in deciding whether to fix bail or to release a defendant without bail. Related legislation set up an agency in the District of Columbia to investigate the background of defendants for bail purposes.

Some judges soon complained that they regretted being "forced" to release criminals. An author of the reform act, Sen. Sam J. Ervin (D N.C.), insisted that it did not force the courts to release anyone. He said a line must be drawn between bail and preventive detention, which had been "illegal since the dawn of American jurisprudence." But the controversy has not been stilled.

"They'll be released on bond and be out on the street before the officer has even finished his paperwork," Assistant D. C. Police Chief Jerry V. Wilson said on Oct. 21, 1968, while testifying before the National Commission on the Causes and Prevention of Violence. Former D. C. Public Safety Director Patrick V. Murphy, appearing before the commission nine days later, said that 45 of 130 persons arrested for robbery in a preceding 12-month period were rearrested and indicted for additional robberies while awaiting trial for the original offense. A federal law enforcement official told Editorial Research Reports that offenders such as these—mostly young—realize they will be found guilty and try to commit as many additional robberies as possible before being sent to prison. Mayor Walter E. Washington announced Jan. 13, 1969, that the District of Columbia government would ask Congress to amend the Bail Reform Act of 1966 to make it possible to hold under detention persons awaiting trial who have been charged with specified types of crime.[14]

---

[14] The Senate Judiciary Subcommittee on Constitutional Rights is to open hearings Jan. 21 on the question of whether the Bail Reform Act has contributed to a sharp increase of crime in the District of Columbia.

Arlen Specter, Philadelphia district attorney, told the National Commission on the Causes and Prevention of Violence, Oct. 30, that there were at that time 350 defendants in cases before state or local courts in Philadelphia who had been charged with a second serious offense while out on bail awaiting trial. Only a fortnight earlier, on Oct. 17, an armed robber and a policeman had been killed during a hold-up attempt in that city. The robber, John Joseph Seeley, was free at the time on $15,000 bail while under indictment on a charge of involuntary manslaughter in the slaying of another policeman a year earlier. When the previous slaying occurred, Seeley was on parole after serving time for robbery, larceny, and firearms violations.

NEED TO SPEED UP TRIALS; JUVENILE COURT REFORM

The dilemma which bail poses for the judge is compounded by long delays in bringing the accused to trial. Delays of a year or more are not uncommon. Chief Justice Warren told an interviewer last autumn that when he leaves the Supreme Court, he wants to devote himself to building up the Federal Judicial Center, an agency created by Congress in 1967 to improve judicial administration in the federal courts. "The most important job of the courts today," Warren said, "is not to decide what the substantive law is, but to work out ways to move the cases along and relieve court congestion."[15]

The dockets would be even more crowded if it were not for the extra-legal practice of "plea bargaining" between the prosecutor and defense attorney—that of reducing the original charge in return for a plea of guilty to a lesser one. Though plea bargaining does not exist in juvenile courts, the President's Crime Commission has noted, the juvenile process can—and often does—involve "extra-judicial negotiations." Juvenile courts have existed in the United States under that name since 1899, but the constitutionality of their procedures was not passed upon by the Supreme Court until May 1967. Then in a test case, *In the Matter of Gault* (383 U.S. 555), Justice Abe Fortas said on behalf of the Court that all "fact-finding" hearings in juvenile courts "must measure up to the essentials of due process and fair treatment." Commenting on the ruling, Columbia University law professor Monrad G. Paulson said it was "built on the premise that the juvenile court system has failed to provide the

---

[15] Quoted by Fred P. Graham, *New York Times*, Sept. 30, 1968. Graham reported that Warren hoped to persuade the states to establish judicial centers to work with the federal center.

care and treatment which the theory underlying it has posited." He described so-called training schools as "often nothing more than prisons for the young." [16]

"Reform of juvenile courts is critical," the late Robert F. Kennedy said in an address to the Columbia Law School Forum, Jan. 19, 1967, "because such a high percentage of crime is committed either by adolescents or by adult offenders who were involved with the law when they were adolescents." A number of studies indicate that more than half of all adult felons had juvenile court records. Since 1961 Congress has financed pilot projects to fight juvenile delinquency, but until 1968, with passage of the Juvenile Delinquency Prevention and Control Act, federal aid for this purpose remained small. That act authorized a three-year $150 million program of grants to states for prevention of youth crime and rehabilitation of young offenders.

SHORTCOMINGS IN PENAL AND CORRECTIONAL SYSTEMS

The entire American correctional and penal system—for juveniles and adults—is judged a failure by a legion of critics. Two-thirds of the men and women now imprisoned are repeaters—inmates who received the prescribed treatment but were not rehabilitated. "Prisons cannot . . . be a reforming influence so long as they are assigned the task of inflicting punishment," an ex-convict, Hal Hollister, wrote in *Harper's* magazine in August 1962. Despite some promising innovations here and there, prisons are looked on as breeding grounds of crime and homosexuality.[17]

Legal scholars contend that prison sentences in the United States tend to be more severe than in any other advanced Western nation. James V. Bennett, former director of the Federal Bureau of Prisons, is trying to enlist citizen support for a movement to curb the disparity of sentences imposed for the same offense in different jurisdictions within the United States. He seeks federal legislation to give U. S. Courts of Appeal power to review sentences which the convicted man alleges to be excessive.

The prison population, in the meantime, is growing larger and younger. The Bureau of Prisons reported in August 1968 that in the previous 12 months the average age of federal

---

[16] Monrad G. Paulson, "The Role of Juvenile Courts," *Current History*, August 1968, p. 74.

[17] See "Rehabilitation of Prisoners," *E.R.R.*, 1965 Vol. II, pp. 743-757.

Street Crime in America

prisoners had dropped from 29 to 28. Dr. Karl Menninger, the psychiatrist, contends that "Society secretly wants crime, needs crime, and gains definite satisfaction from the mishandling of it." It is his belief that "The public has a fascination for violence and clings tenaciously to its yen for vengeance, blind and deaf to the expense, futility, and dangerousness of the resulting penal system." Menninger is convinced that "there is effective treatment for offenders," but he says that "The great majority of offenders, even 'criminals,' should never become prisoners if we want to 'cure' them." [18]

New Efforts to Cut Incidence of Crime

THE CENTRAL CONCLUSION of the President's Crime Commission was that significant reduction in crime was possible despite the inherent difficulties of the problem. It recommended, among other things, the upgrading of state and local police forces, improvement of methods of law enforcement at all levels, and compilation of more accurate and comprehensive crime statistics. Provisions to carry out some of the commission's recommendations were contained in the Crime Control and Safe Streets Act of 1968, which created a Law Enforcement Assistance Administration and a National Institute of Law Enforcement and Criminal Justice. These agencies, both in the Justice Department, were authorized to provide financial and technical assistance to state and local law enforcement agencies.

The theory behind the new law was that the federal government should provide aid but not itself engage directly in local law enforcement. Traditionally, law enforcement has been a state and local function—one which the states guard jealously. A coalition of Republicans and southern Democrats overrode the wishes of the Johnson administration and wrote into the law a provision to channel the federal funds to the states instead of directly to local communities. Reallocation to those communities was left to the states.

The federal-state question surfaced in another way during

---

[18] Karl Menninger, "The Crime of Punishment," *Saturday Review*, Sept. 7, 1968, pp. 21-25 and 55. The article is adapted from Menninger's book of the same name, published in October 1968.

congressional consideration of the measure. City and state police departments, represented in Washington by the International Association of Chiefs of Police, were engaged in behind-the-scenes rivalry with the F.B.I. over whether the additional training of police officers authorized by the act should be controlled by their departments or by the federal agency. In the end, the F.B.I. was empowered to conduct the training in ways and places of its own choosing. The new law also expanded the F.B.I. National Academy, which provides the training, and it authorized the bureau's crime research laboratory to "develop new techniques, systems, equipment and devices to strengthen law enforcement."

President Nixon has proposed establishment of a National Academy of Law Enforcement to train not only policemen but also prosecutors, probation and parole officers, and correctional personnel. It would give college-level training which the F.B.I. academy does not offer. Also proposed by Nixon is a Cabinet-level National Law Enforcement Council to coordinate federal law enforcement activities and oversee the F.B.I. and 25 other federal law enforcement agencies, including the Secret Service, Internal Revenue Service, and the Bureau of Narcotics and Dangerous Drugs.

Of 23,000 federal investigative agents fewer than one-third are in the F.B.I. President Johnson by executive order in 1968 consolidated into the Justice Department the Bureau of Narcotics (then in the Treasury Department) and the Bureau of Drug Abuse Control (then in the Department of Health, Education, and Welfare). Narcotics are widely recognized as a key element in the prevalence of street crime; users rob and steal to buy their drugs. But an exact measurement of the problem awaits fuller statistical reporting.[19]

Today 40,000 law enforcement agencies in the United States, most of them municipal police departments, employ 420,000 men and women and expend about $2.5 billion annually. The agencies vary in size from New York City's police department, with 28,000 members, to one-man departments. The 55 largest cities in the country employ one-fourth of the country's total police manpower.

Big-city police budgets have risen sharply in recent years despite other pressing municipal needs. For example, Detroit

---

[19] See "Control of City Crime," *E.R.R.*, 1961 Vol. II, pp. 757-772, and "Legalization of Marijuana," *E.R.R.*, 1967 Vol. II, pp. 577-596.

police spending went up from $48 million in 1962 to $64 million in 1967. But many police departments still remain below authorized strength, largely because of low pay. The National League of Cities, in a survey of 284 police departments in 1966, found that almost two-thirds of them were undermanned. The President's Crime Commission concluded, however, that there appeared to be little correlation between the police-citizen ratio and the crime rate. Among cities of a half-million people or more, the ratios varied from 1.07 policemen per thousand residents to 4.04, while the incidence of reported crime in those cities showed no great differences.

However, the commission detected a correlation between crime solution and the time it takes for patrol officers to respond to a call. In a Los Angeles study, it was found that the average response time was 4.1 minutes in cases in which arrests were made, and 6.3 minutes in cases in which arrests were not made. The Los Angeles study showed further that one-third of all arrests were effected within half an hour of the time the crime was committed.

CIVILIAN REVIEW BOARDS; COMMUNITY POLICE CONTROL

Police officials hope that federal money will help their cities obtain new equipment to cut the time lag between call and response. New York City, for one, has installed a big computerized communications center. Some cities are experimenting with "putting the cop back on the beat" so that he will get to know neighborhood residents better than he can from a squad car. But there is evidence that much of the money and energy that might be expended for the prevention and detection of everyday street crime is going instead into riot control planning and weaponry. Several big-city police departments were reported last year to be buying arsenals of heavy weapons, including tank-like armored police cars.

Riot-control measures reflect what a number of specialists believe to be a hardening of attitudes between Negro and white communities—attitudes which are reflected in encounters between white policemen and Negroes in the ghettos. Some cities have tried to ease hostility by establishing civilian police-review boards to investigate allegations of police misconduct.

John V. Lindsay came into office as mayor of New York, Jan. 1, 1966, promising to reform the city police department's Civilian Complaint Review Board. There was pressure from civil rights groups and minority spokesmen to widen the civilian representation on the board and make it, in effect, extra-departmental. Vincent Broderick, then the police commissioner, resigned rather than carry out the changes advocated by Lindsay. He was replaced by Howard R. Leary, Philadelphia's police commissioner. Leary, a New York observer wrote, "was a career man, a professional, and yet he had helped establish, or at least gone along with, a civilian-dominated review board in Philadelphia; his cops had behaved well in handling racial disturbances; his reputation was good in the ghettos." [20]

The Patrolmen's Benevolent Association, strongly opposed to the Lindsay plan, succeeded in placing on the November 1966 ballot a referendum question on whether the city should retain a review board at all. Calling the issue a "symbolic gesture" rather than a real solution of police-ghetto problems, Aaron Wildavsky wrote:

> The game begins with a publicity campaign focusing on fascist police, various atrocities, and other lurid events. The police and their friends counter with an equally illuminating defense: nothing is wrong that a little get-tough campaign would not cure. The game ends with a ballot in which white voters are asked to choose between their friendly neighborhood policeman and the specter of black violence. The usual result is that the whites vote for the police and defeat the review board.

"If a review board is created," Wildavsky added, "it soon becomes apparent that a few judgments against policemen have no effect on the critical problem of securing adequate protection for Negroes. But the game is a perfect loser: everyone's feelings are exacerbated and the conflict continues at a new height of hostility." [21]

In Washington, a coalition of Negro militants known as the Black United Front demanded that the D. C. government let local neighborhoods elect "Selection and Review Boards" to appoint precinct captains and all their subordinates, set standards for their behavior and hear citizen complaints against the police. The City Council held a hearing Nov. 25,

---

[20] Richard Dougherty, "How Leary Has Managed to Survive," *New York* magazine, Aug. 5, 1968, p. 26.

[21] Aaron Wildavsky, "Recipe for Violence," *New York*, May 20, 1968, p. 28. See also "Negroes and the Police," *E.R.R.*, 1964 Vol. II, pp. 681-700.

1968, on a modified plan which would permit the mayor to appoint "community advisory boards." Board members would interview all policemen coming into a precinct and those eligible for promotion. A Negro member of the council, William S. Thompson, said the precinct captains would give "reasonable and appropriate adherence" to the advice of the boards. But a spokesman for the Black United Front, Reginald H. Booker, was quoted by newsmen as saying at the council hearing: "Every black person in the room should get a gun. . . . Our objective is to wipe out white cops."

VIGILANTE GROUPS AND NEW GUN CONTROL LEGISLATION

In reaction to violent rhetoric of that sort, numerous white people on the fringes of the ghetto—and sometimes far out into the suburbs—have proceeded to arm themselves. In some instances, whites have banded together into "protective associations" and the like. In New Jersey, the Newark North Ward Citizens Committee was formed after riots occurred in that city in 1967; since then, chapters have been established in some nearby suburban communities. Members own guns and patrol in radio-equipped cars. To Anthony Imperiale, the Newark organizer and leader, they are "defenders of law and order;" to Gov. Richard J. Hughes of New Jersey they are "vigilantes." [22]

In Orlando, Fla., some 2,400 women formed a "Pistol Packing Posse" in the fall of 1966 after a series of rapes occurred in that city. Orlando police, fearing that citizens might be more endangered by amateur gun handlers than by rapists, set up a free course in the proper use of firearms. Police officials need the help of citizens in controlling street crime, but they note that organized citizen groups have a habit of turning into vigilantes.

Congress in 1968 enacted firearms-control legislation for the first time since it had outlawed the interstate transport of sawed-off shotguns three decades earlier. The Crime Control and Safe Streets Act prohibits the interstate shipment of pistols and revolvers to individuals and the over-the-counter purchase of handguns by individuals who do not live in the dealer's state. Under public pressure following the assassinations of Martin Luther King Jr. and Robert F. Kennedy, Congress adopted separate legislation banning most out-of-state purchases of rifles, shotguns, handguns

---

[22] Quoted by Paul Goldberger, "Tony Imperiale Stands Vigilant for Lawandorder," *New York Times Magazine,* Sept. 29, 1968, p. 30.

and ammunition. It stopped short, however, of acting on President Johnson's request for legislation to require registration and licensing of privately owned firearms. Johnson in his valedictory address called the failure to enact such a measure "one of my greatest disappointments." He said: "I think if we had passed that act, it would have reduced the incidence of crime, and I believe that Congress should adopt such a law, and I hope that it will at a not too distant date."

The President's Crime Commission noted that 268 of the 278 law enforcement officers slain from 1960 to 1965 were killed by firearms. The National Commission on the Causes and Prevention of Violence reported, Oct. 9, 1968, that 1.2 million handguns were produced in the United States or imported during the first half of the year, more than three times as many as during the entire year 1951.

PUBLIC COMPENSATION FOR THE VICTIMS OF CRIME

The inability of government to protect citizens from crime has given rise in recent years, here and abroad, to proposals for compensating the victims of crime. New Zealand adopted a compensation plan in 1963, and Britain did the same in 1964. California established the first such program in the United States, effective at the beginning of 1966, and New York followed suit later the same year. The New York law applies only to victims who suffer "serious financial hardship" but still is considered more liberal in its benefits than the California law. The *Los Angeles Times* reported Feb. 19, 1967, that only 32 California crime victims had been compensated up to that time, in a total amount of $56,620.

Sen. Yarborough has introduced bills in Congress to make federal funds available to pay hospital expenses and losses of income suffered by crime victims in federal jurisdictions, but no action has been taken on the proposed legislation. One reason is that police studies indicate that the victim of a crime frequently instigates the violence—or contributes to it in some way. Marital disputes, for example, account for a sizable share of criminal violence. F.B.I. records show that one policeman in five killed in the line of duty was trying to break up a family fight.[23] Statistics such as these make it plain that crime is filled with anomalies that defy easy correction.

---

[23] See "Compensation for Victims of Crime," *E.R.R.*, 1965 Vol. II, pp. 685-700.

DISCIPLINE IN PUBLIC SCHOOLS

by

Helen B. Shaffer

1 9 6 9
Aug. 27

DISCIPLINE IN PUBLIC SCHOOLS

THE NATION'S public schools are about to open their doors to what is likely to be their most critical year for disciplinary management since the schoolmaster put away the birch rod. The private schools will have their troubles, too, but they are still in position to pick and choose, to suspend and expel, as they see fit, and they are not so hemmed in by bureaucratic controls nor so harassed by conflicting pressures. The public schools, holding a mandate for mass education but possessed of inadequate resources and involved in social crises beyond their control, are in for a rough time, and most of their teachers and administrators know it. The trouble is complex, pervasive, many-faceted; the most immediate problem before the educators can be summed up in two words: student unrest.

Student disorders during the 1968-69 school year gave warning of what to expect in the year ahead. Trouble was not confined to crowded and decaying schools of the inner city; it struck repeatedly at country and suburban schools as well. Long before the term ended in June, it had become clear that the crack in the authority structure of American education, first opened on college campuses, had spread down into senior and junior high schools and even reached into elementary schools. Concern over the situation currently centers on the secondary schools. A high-ranking official of the Department of Health, Education and Welfare told newsmen, Aug. 20, that a diminution of disorder on college campuses was expected this autumn but that the prospect of rising violence in senior and junior high schools remained.

A new assertiveness, incredibly brazen by standards of the past, has obviously taken hold of the adolescent captives of the compulsory education system. Some adults cheer it, many deplore it; the consensus seems to be that it has aspects both good and bad. Youth's concern for the quality of education and for peace and justice raises few com-

87

plaints. But its contempt for authority and its roughshod manner of expressing grievances are unsettling, almost frightening to the elders of school and community. Even when motivated by youthful idealism, the challenge to authority thrown down by young militants has helped to create an atmosphere in many schools conducive to the release of aggressive impulses of less benign origin.

Violence in the schools has been a particularly ominous development. Vandalism, assaults on teachers, and warfare between student factions have increased. The principal of a high school in the Bronx section of New York City told an educators' meeting in March 1969 that "my faculty are fearful of actual physical violence" and "parents call almost daily, reporting attacks on their children."[1] The High School Principals Association of that city had appealed to the Mayor and the Board of Education in January for help to meet a crisis; "disorders and fears of new and frightening dimensions stalk the corridors of our schools," the association said. ". . . The hour is late, our schools are in peril." New York City School Superintendent Bernard E. Donovan on March 16 directed every junior and senior high school to name a security official, and he stationed trained security aides in the troubled schools.

School authorities in other large cities have likewise taken emergency action to curb outbreaks of student violence. Police or armed guards have been placed in schools in many cities—Chicago, Flint, Mich., Harrisburg, Pa., Kansas City, Newark, Oakland, Philadelphia, and others. The Toledo City Council on April 21 adopted an ordinance, described as an "emergency measure," prescribing special penalties for persons convicted of assaulting teachers or students, of disrupting or interfering with educational activities, or of using "improper, indecent or profane" language to a teacher.[2]

Teachers in big-city schools may well remember 1968-69 as the year when hazards of the profession became serious enough to inject the question of "combat pay" into discussions of public school salaries. The American Federation of Teachers rejected "the ugly concept of combat pay" when

---

[1] C. Edwin Linville, "New Directions in Secondary Education" (address at convention of National Association of Secondary School Principals, San Francisco, Feb. 28-March 5, 1969), *The Bulletin* (of the N.A.S.S.P.), May 1969, p. 205.

[2] The maximum penalty for assault was fixed at $1,000 fine or one year in prison; for bad language, $300 or 30 days.

it was suggested in congressional debate that federal funds might properly be made available for that purpose. An editorial in the union newspaper asserted that such payments would be equivalent to "a bribe to teach in a ghetto school," and that they would stigmatize the school in the minds of students and parents. But a Brooklyn teacher retorted that "combat pay . . . [was] justified" by conditions in the "ghetto school." [3]

It may not be coincidental that in the autumn of 1969 members of the leading national high school principals' association will be offered coverage under a new "Educators' Professional Liability Policy" that will provide benefits of up to $300,000 for personal injury, and similar protection against liability for injury to others, as well as $500 for bail bond and $2,000 for legal expenses. This development and a trend toward extending similar insurance coverage to teachers under statewide plans reflect the increase in litigation over school issues, which is another facet of the upheaval in the schools and the challenge to traditional authority in the disciplining of students.

STUDENT ACTIVISM AS MAJOR SOURCE OF DISORDER

The active concern of students over school questions, or about public issues of the day, has led in many cases to school disorders and a challenging of disciplinary procedures. "To ignore student activism in 1970," the principal of a Wilmington, Del., high school said at a recent seminar for school administrators, "is to invite total chaos in a school." [4] Another big-city high school principal observed that "To be a principal in times like these is not for the faint-hearted and we're just getting started on this protest business." According to the National Association of Secondary Principals, to whom the latter remark was addressed, such statements are echoes of "what principals are saying across the nation, in the poverty-ridden cities or prosperous suburbs—and even in rural communities."

This assessment was based on the returns from a questionnaire the association sent in January 1969 to a national sample of high school principals. Of 1,026 who replied, 606 or 59 per cent reported that there had been some kind of

---

[3] *American Teacher*, May 1969, p. 4, and June 1969, p. 2.

[4] Quoted in report of Institute for Development of Educational Activities, Inc. (I/D/E/A) on its 1969 Fellows Summer Institutes for School Administrators, held July 7-12, 1969, on four college campuses.

student activism in their schools, and many who had not yet experienced it said they expected it in the near future. Urban and suburban schools showed no difference in the prevalence of activism; in each group the incidence was 67 per cent as against 53 per cent in large and small rural schools taken as a single group. Large suburban schools (more than 2,000 students) were the most affected; 81 per cent of them reported student activism, as did 74 per cent of the large urban schools. Even among the least affected, the small rural schools, fully 50 per cent reported activism of some kind.[5]

"One of the surprises of the survey," N.A.S.S.P.'s researchers reported, "was the fact that protest is almost as likely to occur in junior . . . as in senior high schools." Three-fifths of the urban and suburban junior high schools reported protest activity. "Student activism is the subject of the hour," the report stated. ". . . Everyone has an opinion on it." Targets of the protests were numerous: a large number concerned dress and grooming rules, but approximately one-fourth of the total involved race relations, the peace movement, or the draft. Significantly, 45 per cent of the schools with activist experience reported attacks on the character of the educational program; more than four-fifths of the large urban senior high school protests were in that area.

Student activism gained momentum during the school year. A monitoring of 1,800 daily newspapers by the Center for Research and Education at Columbia University showed a tripling of the frequency of disturbances over a four-month period, November 1968 - February 1969. This study, which was carried out under contract with the U. S. Office of Education, showed that 348 schools in 38 states experienced disruptions in the four-month period and that 239 of the disruptions were "serious episodes" like strikes, sit-ins, riots, or other forms of violence.

The onset of spring brought a seasonal rise. Dr. Alan F. Westin, director of the Center survey, estimated in May that at least 2,000 high schools in the nation had suffered disruptions. In some of the larger cities, a majority of high schools had serious outbreaks at some time during the school

---

[5] J. Lloyd Trump, Associate Secretary, and Jane Hunt, editorial assistant, of National Association of Secondary School Principals, report presented at San Francisco convention, Feb. 28 - March 5, 1969.

year. *The Urban Crisis Monitor,* put out by the Urban Research Council in Chicago, said in May 1969 that any survey made at that time "would show a sharp increase in protests in high schools."

INFLUENCE OF NEW LEFT IN SECONDARY SCHOOLS

The mood in the high schools has encouraged a growth of juvenile radicalism of the New Left variety. The Students for a Democratic Society, which started on college campuses, has been trying to recruit members in the high schools. They have had the greatest success in high schools located near college campuses, which supply many of the organizers for the movement. Michael Klonsky, S.D.S. national secretary, said recently that the average age of S.D.S. members was getting lower. "Our biggest growth," he said, "has been among high school and junior high school students." [6]

The S.D.S. published in 1967 a treatise on how to "take over" a high school. This document, *High School Reform: Toward a Student Movement,* was written in 1965 by a Los Angeles high school student and has served to guide organizers of radical movements in the schools. It suggests ways in which minor student grievances can be escalated into major protest demonstrations. One of its recommendations is to establish an underground newspaper in which students can freely express gripes against the "system."

Whether or not the adolescent Machiavellis of the S.D.S. were influential in the matter, the 1968-69 school year was marked by an unprecedented growth of juvenile journalism, carried on without the guiding hand of a faculty adviser and aping the style, content and format of underground papers put out by older anti-establishment youths. Estimates of the number of underground high school papers rose from 500 early in the year to around 1,000 by the time the spring semester was drawing to a close. The papers were serviced by their own national news service, known as HIPS (High School Independent Press Service), with headquarters in New York.

The underground papers tend to sustain the mood of warfare between the school as authority ("jail-keepers") and

---

6 "Nothing Administrators Can Do Is Right," an interview with Michael Klonsky, *I/D/E/A Reporter,* Spring Quarter 1969, p. 67. According to *I/D/E/A Reporter,* a publication of the Institute for Development of Educational Activities, the S.D.S. leader demanded a fee for the interview and said he would not have granted it at all except that he was very low on funds.

the victim-students ("prisoners"). "The papers attack the despotism of the principal, the dullness and incompetence of teachers by name, and the irrelevance and the reactionary nature of the curriculum," the principal of a high school in the Bronx said in an address to his colleagues. "They extol the glories of 'pot,' . . . give advice on sex and birth-control, . . . [and] recruit for demonstrations." [7] A somewhat more sympathetic account of the high school underground papers describes them as "fresh, crazy, biased, irreverent, . . . and often unexpectedly inventive." The papers "talk with the authority of the insider about the follies of the institution and the ways it might be undermined or openly confronted." The more "seasoned" papers "operate confidently on the understanding that change in the schools is their first order of business." [8]

One of the ways in which the underground paper serves the radical movement is to provide the occasion for a confrontation and for escalation of conflict. This occurs when a school disciplines a student for selling a paper on school premises without authorization. A large number of students may then be moved to protest the disciplinary action as a violation of the students' right of access to the paper. Punitive action has been taken by a number of schools against underground paper sellers who have refused to desist when so ordered. In some cases the action was taken in response to pressure by conservative elements in the community.

DAMAGE TO BUILDINGS AND EQUIPMENT BY VANDALS

Perhaps the most difficult aspect of the disciplinary problem is the general feeling of hostility toward school and the "system" which apparently underlies much of the disorderly and disruptive behavior of today's students. Such hostility appears among bright students as well as slow learners, among children from comfortable homes who have "everything going for them" as well as children who live in the most deprived circumstances; among students in new, well-equipped, relatively uncrowded schools and students in derelict, overcrowded, understaffed schools in poor districts.

Anger at the school or indifference to its welfare accounts for the rising toll of vandalism. The U. S. Office of Education has estimated that damage done by vandals to public schools

---

[7] C. Edwin Linville, *op. cit.*, p. 204.
[8] Diane Divoky, "The Way It's Going to Be," *Saturday Review*, Feb. 15, 1969, p. 89.

across the country adds up to as much as $100 million a year. A survey conducted by Baltimore school officials showed that vandalism in 1967-68 cost the public schools $2.7 million in New York City; $940,100 in Los Angeles; $716,600 in Baltimore; $683,500 in Tampa; $535,000 in Boston; $410,500 in the District of Columbia; $407,000 in Milwaukee; $346,400 in Newark; $309,000 in Oakland; and $253,800 in Kansas City.

Much of the damage consists of window breakage from rock throwing, a familiar form of schoolboy mischief which the schools have long had to contend with but never to such a degree. Even more ominous are outbreaks of pupil rioting—rampages through school corridors, the smashing of furniture and equipment, overturning of office machines and files, setting of fires, etc. The monetary cost of damage so caused, including the rise in insurance rates that results, is the least of the problems. The sheer nihilism of such acts baffles school authorities, widens the breach between school and student, and injects an atmosphere of guerrilla warfare into the schoolhouse, vastly complicating the educator's task.

Schools, of course, are not the only targets affected by the increased incidence of vandalism. But school-age children are responsible for a large percentage of all willful destruction of property, private as well as public. Perhaps nothing else so dramatically underlines the weakening that has been taking place in the authority of schools to enforce student discipline.

Weakening of Authority Over Pupils

A BODY OF PRINCIPLES on student discipline, developed by American education over the past half-century or longer, appeared until recently to satisfy nearly everyone as reasonable, humane, educationally productive and eminently suited to the goals of a democratic society. Almost overnight, the entire edifice of institutionalized procedures, developed to implement the principles, came under attack and students themselves were prominent among the attackers. Suddenly the rules on discipline in the standard teachers' manuals became, if not obsolete, at least not pertinent to the instant problems presented by unorthodox student behavior. Teachers who were taught how to deal with long-familiar types of difficult kids—the class clown, the back-talker, the unwilling worker, etc.—found themselves facing a new breed of misbehavers: rebels who challenged the entire institutional structure that supported the authority of the teacher and the principal.

The challengers were not mere deviants from the norm, the "bad boy" or "bad girl" who is likely to appear in any class and who can be singled out for special disciplinary action. Often they were junior authority figures themselves, capable of calling on a large sympathetic constituency in the classroom and even beyond it. The young rebel's supporters might include parents, preachers, politicians, even teachers. In Washington, D. C., militant black students found a sympathizer on the school board who encouraged their use of disruptive tactics to gain their ends.

INAPPLICABILITY OF OLD DISCIPLINARY RULES TODAY

A student rule-breaker of this kind can scarcely be dealt with effectively by a reproof from his teacher or by the issuance of a detention hall slip. In a classroom confrontation the young disrupter of the educational process may have a better grasp of strategy than his teacher. He may counter an effort to discipline him by leading a sit-in, organizing a class boycott, or going to court to establish his legal rights. In the atmosphere that prevails in many schools today, what begins as an ordinary case of misbehavior may blow up into a full-scale disorder. Police have been called and schools shut down for trouble that began when a teacher sought to discipline a pupil for a minor rule infraction.

This is particularly true in schools where there are tensions based on race. Racial unrest in senior and junior high schools results from "long-brewing black resentments against racism," the Urban Research Council in Chicago noted last May. "Almost always the triggering incident is minor and innocuous in itself." The sensitivity of minority race students to real or imagined prejudice in school personnel or in the application of disciplinary procedures adds immeasurably to the inflammatory possibilities. The teacher or principal, in his efforts to carry out normal disciplinary procedures, may be accused either of disciplining the black student too severely out of prejudice or of disciplining him too leniently in order to avoid a charge of prejudice.

But the new breed of student may be white or black, rich or poor. "The most visible trend of secondary education today," said the principal of a high school in the Bronx which was the scene of considerable trouble during the past school year, "is the change in our students":

> Language becomes harsher and profanity is now coeducational. A subtle kind of defiant posture masks the normal tendencies of adolescents to be cheerful and cooperative. Absenteeism and cutting have mushroomed. The new breed of parent glories in the individualism of the child. . . . Narcotics invade the most respectable of our high schools, and marijuana is obviously in high fashion among the most sophisticated and intellectual of the young.
>
> High school students are eager to catch up with college students. The apathy we used to deplore is now replaced by acute social consciousness.

To deal with the new breed requires not only patience but also "an open-minded commitment to explore new directions, freed from the shackles of the conventional wisdom, and from the inertia of the status quo." [9]

PAST RELIANCE ON FEAR OF CORPORAL PUNISHMENT

Teachers in the more difficult schools may long at times for the autocratic methods of keeping order and forcing obedience that were available to schoolmasters in earlier times. But even if today's students would submit to the harsher disciplines of the past, these methods would hardly suit the goals of modern education. The old disciplinary procedures served a society that held submission to authority to be a prime goal of childhood education. Today the ideal product of the mass schooling system is expected to possess an independent mind and a cooperative spirit, traits not likely to flourish in an atmosphere of institutional coercion.

For most of the years of American education, fear of the rod was a major instrument of student discipline. Infliction of physical pain was justified on the same grounds as were the harsh penal codes of the day for adults. "Fear was conceived as the only force which would make men amenable to dominion. . . . It was natural [to believe] that children, too, should be controlled by violence or the threat of violence." [10]

An historian of childhood, Philippe Aries, has traced the great change in educational style that took place between

---

[9] C. Edwin Linville, *op. cit.*, p. 203.
[10] Herbert Arnold Falk, *Corporal Punishment: A Social Interpretation of Its Theory and Practice in the Schools of the United States* (1941), p. 3.

the late Middle Ages and the 17th century, from a com-
radely association of teachers and learners to prisonlike
schools where "the birch became the mark of the schoolmaster, . . . the symbol of the subjection in which [he] . . .
held his pupils." [11] The authoritarian school was the product
of an authoritarian society, the power of the schoolmaster
over pupils reflecting the power of the king over his subjects.
And where authority became absolute, harsh penalties to
uphold it usually followed. Thus "a humiliating disciplinary
system—whipping at the masters' discretion, . . . became
widespread" in the schools of France and England. The
American colonists, coming from a land where flogging had
become common in schools, took it for granted that corporal
punishment would be used to control children in the schools
they established in the New World.

The child in pre-Revolutionary America suffered not only
pain of the flesh but the tormenting threat of eternal dam-
nation. A catechism told him he would be "sent down to
everlasting fire" if he were naughty. Evangelist preachers
told him children were born sinful and graphically described
what awaited them in the afterworld. "This repressive attitude toward life, this insistence on conformity to a moral
and ethical code based on purely religious sanction, was
naturally reflected in the colonial schools and in the discipline of children." [12]

The libertarian ideas and the humanitarian movements
of the 18th and 19th centuries were slow to overcome the
authoritarian spirit that prevailed in schooling of the young.
Though whipping posts and other harsh instruments of adult
punishment gradually disappeared, "the tradition of the rod
remained fixed in the educational practice." [13] The Rev.
Francis Wayland, president of Brown University, expressed
the prevailing view in a public address in 1830: "The pupil
. . . [is] the inferior. . . . [He is] under the obligation of
obedience, respect and reverence. . . . It is the duty of the
instructor to enforce obedience and of the pupil to render it."

Even Horace Mann, who crusaded during the 1830s
against excessive application of corporal punishment, did
not approve of abolishing it altogether. Another educator,
lecturing in 1843, said: "With the present conditions of

---

[11] Philippe Aries, *Centuries of Childhood* (First Vintage Edition, 1965), pp. 245-258.
[12] Herbert Arnold Falk, *op. cit.*, p. 42.
[13] *Ibid.*, p. 48.

society . . . there are cases in which the good of a school and the good of the offender . . . demand a severe application of the rod. Some teachers may use it . . . too frequently. In our attempt to prevent this, let us not rush to an opposite and equally pernicious extreme." [14]

The pros and cons of corporal punishment were extensively debated in the decades following the Civil War, but its use persisted. A record kept in Boston in 1889 showed 11,768 cases of officially reported physical punishments in boys' grammar schools, which then had a pupil population of 16,198. A number of writers who grew up in the 19th century recalled in memoirs the numerous cruelties inflicted on them for offenses that would be considered trivial, if offenses at all, today—squirming, nervous giggling, whispering, slowness to come forth with the right answer. Ears were twisted or boxed, noses pinched, skulls rapped with a thimbled finger; children were closeted, tethered, made to wear neck yokes that hampered their head movements, and ordered to hold uncomfortable positions until their muscles became cramped. The physical conditions in many schools made it all the more difficult to abide by the universal rule of the schoolroom to sit still and be silent until called on. [15]

Corporal punishment never quite dies as an educational issue. The rise in juvenile delinquency in the decade following World War II revived public support for it. A scholarly study of corporal punishment in the early 1960s showed it was "still a factor in the schools," that "it is still practiced even in areas where regulations forbid it." The author found a "strong trend" of public opinion "away from the permissive and toward the authoritarian point of view in discipline of pupils in the public schools." This was due to concern over "ever-mounting unruliness and disorder in the schools." [16] However, corporal punishment hardly presents itself as an answer to the disciplinary problems of the schools today.

PROGRESSIVE EDUCATION'S APPROACH TO DISCIPLINE

Vast social changes which took place in the early decades of the 20th century modified considerably the authoritarian atmosphere of the public school classroom. The teacher was still "boss" but the prevailing principle on discipline leaned

---

[14] Charles Northend, quoted by Herbert Arnold Falk, *op. cit.*, p. 69.

[15] A School Committee report of 1868 described the schools of Cambridge, Mass., as overcrowded, unventilated "hotbeds of consumption."

[16] Keith Franklin James, *Corporal Punishment in the Public Schools* (1963), pp. 88-89.

more toward cultivation of self-discipline than toward rigid conformity to specific rules of conduct. Advances in the study of child psychology and the measurement of intelligence, growing recognition of emotional factors in learning, the rising influence of the scientific spirit, and the declining influence of Puritan morality over public education all helped to free the student from the stern discipline of earlier days.

Loosening of controls over student life was apparent in the growth of student councils, the provision of playgrounds and other recreational facilities, the institution of elective courses, and the decline in adherence to the punishment principle as an aid to learning. New guidelines on student discipline were embodied in the progressive education movement, which became increasingly influential in the post-World War I era. Progressive education held: "The conduct of the pupil should be governed by himself according to the social needs of his community, rather than by arbitrary laws. Full opportunity for initiative and self-expression should be provided."[17]

John Dewey, high priest of progressive education, described the shift of direction: "To imposition from above is opposed expression and cultivation of individuality; to external discipline is opposed free activity; to learning from texts and teachers, learning through experience." The "external authority" of the teacher was not rejected, Dewey explained; it was rather a question of finding "a more effective source of authority" than imposing facts and rules of conduct on the young.[18] This statement, made in 1938, might well sum up the problem of school discipline today.

New Concept of Students' Rights; Court Tests

Something new has been injected into the turmoil in the schools, something which is likely ultimately to have an important effect on the entire question of student discipline. This is the concept of students' rights. As used by students today, the phrase can mean anything from their right to wear their hair as they please to the exercise of a student veto over the school's instructional program. In the main, however, "students' rights" constitutes the rallying cry of a

---

[17] From *Progressive Education*, April 1924, reprinted in *Readings in American Educational History*, Edgar W. Knight and Clifton L. Hall, eds. (1951), p. 528.

[18] *Ibid.*, p. 535.

crusade against what remains of the autocratic spirit in the public schools as it affects the life of the student.

Much of the students' rights crusade is directed at freeing the high school pupil from pettifogging regulations that routinize his day, deprive him of small freedoms, and subject him to nuisance penalties for infractions of what the pupil considers "stupid" rules. The students' rights movement has also challenged the arbitrary right of the school to suspend or expel students—a punishment more fearful for many of today's college-bound students than a birching at the hands of an old-fashioned schoolmaster—for offenses which students do not consider offenses at all. Still another important direction of the crusade is toward the demand for a more "relevant" education, that is, the provision of courses and the reform of instructional programs to bring them more closely into line with student interests.

What students' rights will come to mean in actual fact is currently in process of formulation, in part through action of the courts and in part through responses of school authorities to student demands. In an address to the seminars on student activism sponsored in July 1969 by the Institute for Development of Educational Activities, A. Edgar Benton, Denver attorney, advised school administrators that students' legal rights were not clear cut. So long as students remain "inactive, nonassertive, submissive, . . . conforming, . . .," he said, "the question of student rights will never come up." Obviously, that happy day is over for many school administrators. To an increasing extent, students and their parents are raising the issue by taking legal action against disciplinary penalties imposed by the schools.

The courts used to uphold school officials unless their action could be proved arbitrary, capricious, or based on faulty information. The *in loco parentis* principle—giving schools the right to exercise their judgment as parents would in disciplining children—prevailed. Recent decisions have moved away from that principle and toward a more positive definition of the student's rights under the Constitution.

The U. S. Supreme Court on Feb. 24, 1969, struck a major blow for students' rights by reversing a lower court decision upholding suspension of two junior high school pupils in Des Moines.[19] The two had been disciplined for wearing black

---

[19] Tinker *v.* Des Moines-Independent Community School District.

armbands, signifying their opposition to the war in Viet
Nam, in defiance of a school rule prohibiting the wearing
of badges or emblems without permission. If the school had
been able to demonstrate that wearing the armbands caused
disorder or disruption of school activities, the decision might
have gone differently. But the High Court held that in the
absence of such evidence, the "undifferentiated fear or
apprehension of disturbance" on the part of school administrators was insufficient reason for denying the students what
was in effect an exercise of their right to free speech under
the First Amendment. Neither students nor teachers "shed
their constitutional rights to freedom of speech or expression at the schoolhouse gate," the Court said.[20]

The trend of lower court decisions also is in the direction
of protecting students' rights and requiring school officials
to justify disciplinary rules as pertinent to the school's educational function. A Superior Court in California found in
1966, for example, that dress regulations must be based on
considerations of student health or safety or the orderly
conduct of school business, not on the mere desire of school
authorities to enforce conformity with particular standards
of propriety. An Alabama court ordered reinstatement of a
student editor who had been removed from his post for dis-
obeying a rule forbidding publication of editorials critical
of the state governor and legislature. Other decisions have
forbidden search of students' lockers or cars without a
search warrant. Summary dismissal of a student without a
hearing can be interpreted as failure to observe due process
of law. "In short, the courts are rapidly beginning to define
the rights of students and the limits of legitimate disciplinary authority for the school official."[21]

The American Civil Liberties Union spelled out in detail
the rights of high school students (and teachers) in a pamphlet, *Academic Freedom in the Secondary Schools,* published in September 1968. Eight amendments to the U. S.
Constitution (First, Fourth, Fifth, Sixth, Seventh, Eighth,
Ninth, and 14th) were found applicable. The pamphlet constitutes a guide to the new freedom in public schools.

---

[20] The Court's opinion was written by former Associate Justice Abe Fortas. Associate Justice Hugo L. Black said in a dissenting opinion that the decision virtually
transferred power to control pupils from the schools to the courts. He predicted that
"After the Court's holding today . . . some students . . . in all schools will be ready,
able, and willing to defy their teachers on practically all orders." This was particularly unfortunate, Black added, because "Groups of students all over the land are
already running loose, conducting break-ins, sit-ins, lie-ins, and smash-ins."

[21] "The School and the Courts," *I/D/E/A Reporter,* Spring Quarter 1969, p. 2.

Response of Schools to New Challenge

AMERICAN SCHOOLMEN appear to be urgently searching for new ways to turn off, or to redirect into more manageable channels, the rising flow of youthful antagonism to the status quo in public education. There have been, and apparently will continue to be, a host of educators' conferences— national, regional, local—dealing with the problem of student unrest and the weakening of standard disciplinary controls. The session with this theme was by far the best attended of 46 group discussions held during the seven-day convention of the National Association of Secondary School Principals in San Francisco, Feb. 28 - March 5, 1969—"a good indicator of how concerned principals are about this problem," the association reported.[22]

The National Education Association recently published a collection of articles from its journal on classroom discipline. Although many of the articles were written before disruptions reached the 1968-69 level, they were republished because "student unrest [is] spreading downward to many high schools" and "maintaining pupil discipline is one of the most persistent problems teachers face."[23] Several N.E.A. organizations—the Association for Supervision and Curriculum Development and the National Committee on Secondary Education—sponsored meetings or seminars on student unrest last April.

GUIDELINES FOR DEALING WITH STUDENT DISRUPTION

The Institute for Development of Educational Activities plans to publish around Oct. 1 a handbook on student activism prepared from material developed at the four seminars it sponsored earlier in the year for administrators of schools in various parts of the country.[24] N.E.A.'s National Center for Human Relations is scheduled to meet in October with teams—that is, groups representing various segments of a school community—from a number of schools which have had serious trouble. From the experiences of these

---

[22] "Ring Around the Convention," *The Bulletin* (of the National Association of Secondary School Principals), May-June 1969, p. xvii.

[23] National Education Association, *Discipline in the Classroom* (1969), p. vii.

[24] The seminars were held July 7-12 on the campuses of four colleges: Mills (Calif.), Southern Utah, Milford (S.C.), and Rockford (Ill.). The institute, better known as I/D/E/A, is an affiliate of the Charles F. Kettering Foundation; it has offices in Dayton, Los Angeles, and Melbourne, Fla.

schools, it is hoped to develop guidelines for meeting the problem of student dissent in constructive ways.

High school principals, so often the chief target of student disruptions, have been particularly active in preparing for the expected onslaught in the 1969-70 school year. The principal is in a particularly difficult position because he must not only take the brunt of the student protests, but also contend with rising militancy among teachers and parents, who often disagree among themselves on what should be done. With student unions pressing for reform on one side and ad hoc "Concerned Parents" organizations pressing conservative positions on the other, the principal is "clearly the man in the middle," as the executive secretary of the National Association of Secondary School Principals put it in his annual report last spring.

"As you well know," the Ohio Association of Secondary School Principals wrote in a message to its members in May, "it is becoming increasingly difficult to operate the public schools." The message accompanied a "position statement . . . on student unrest" and a copy of a sample "Resolution Supporting Teachers and School Administrators," suggested for adoption by boards of education. A number of boards, it was said, had adopted such resolutions. That they were needed was sufficient commentary on the shaken authority of the principals.

The national high school principals' association expects to publish this autumn a report on a study that probably will be of use to its members in coping with problems of student unrest. The study, conducted by Dr. Kenneth Fish, principal of the Montclair (N. J.) High School,[25] included analyses of the situation in 15 selected high schools, including some which had as many as 100 policemen patrolling their corridors, and others where there had been no trouble "even though the ingredients of conflict" were present—"bigness, urban location and a racially mixed population." Dr. Fish has already offered the nation's high school principals a number of "tentative" recommendations:

> Muster in advance of conflict the resources of faculty, administration, student body, and community in cooperative efforts to resolve differences.
>
> Communicate, continuously and fully, with students.

---

[25] The Ford Foundation and the Montclair, N. J., Board of Education are co-sponsors with N.A.S.S.P. of the study.

Make needed reforms in student council.
Expand activities program.
Call for and use outside help when needed.
Develop an emergency plan.
Work positively with news media.
Reform the curriculum.[26]

The N.A.S.S.P. is expected to draw up a position paper on student unrest, based on findings of this study.

TREND TOWARD REFORM OF EDUCATIONAL PROGRAMS

On the whole, public school administrators who have been through the fire of student unrest evince considerable willingness to meet the more reasonable demands of young militants and to give students the greater responsibility that the new freedom entails. A number of schools have relented on dress and grooming, allowing students to set their own standards within general bounds of modesty and cleanliness. Freedom of the press is also being extended to the innovative journalists of the high schools with only the stipulation that they skip the obscenities and libelous attacks on individuals.

To reach an accommodation in the case of student demands for a share in control of the instructional program presents a more difficult problem, but many of the student complaints about "irrelevant curriculums" are only echoes of what has been said for years by educators and school administrators. Criticism of public school education in its every aspect has been flowing steadily from the education "establishment"; it fills the professional journals and is sounded repeatedly from the numerous platforms of the education fraternity. "Today's schools fail the middle class as much as they fail the deprived and the affluent," Dr. J. Lloyd Trump, associate secretary of the national high school principals' association, said in a typical utterance of this kind before a meeting of school administrators in July 1969. "The present school curriculum emphasizes content and skills that many pupils neither need nor want."

RECEPTIVITY OF EDUCATORS TO DISCIPLINARY CHANGES

Many schoolmen sympathize with the student challenge of what they consider an obsolete disciplinary system. It was not a student activist or the editor of an underground news-

---

[26] "Montclair Principal Studies Unrest," *NASSP News Letter*, May-June 1969, p. 1.

paper, but the superintendent of the Rockford, Ill., schools who said in an address to fellow educators last May:

> Our schools are organized on a semi-prison approach. We have lack of trust, sign-in and sign-out slips, detention systems, wardens and jailers, fear of escape, regimentation, limited opportunities for choice, barricaded or locked toilet rooms, cell-like classrooms. Why are we surprised that some youngsters rebel? Is it not surprising that more of them do not? [27]

The road to reform is not expected to be easy. Conflict on many fronts is inevitable. A New York teachers' union local, which has called on union leaders around the country to develop "plans of action to deal with disorders in the high school," has criticized school officials "who out of fear or guilt . . . seek to find answers in accommodation to . . . antidemocratic behavior. . . ."[28] The New York Civil Liberties Union attacked the New York Principals' Association report for having "lumped together" student vandalism and assaults with activities like "peaceful distribution of political literature."

The national secretary of the Students for a Democratic Society told an interviewer that nothing a school administrator could do to appease student radicals would satisfy them because the whole system was oppressive; that "administrators oppress young people"; and that "whether they do that liberally or conservatively, they are still doing it."[29] And a Concerned Parents Association of a high school in Arlington, Va., called on parents on Aug. 5 to mobilize against efforts of radical militants to "introduce new procedures into the educational system . . . under the guise of personal 'freedoms' of speech, press, assembly, appearance, conduct and behavior."

These are only some of the aspects of the conflicts that lie ahead in the struggle for acceptance of new modes of maintaining student discipline. The consensus is that changes will come about nonetheless, and that when the schools have actually become better adjusted to the needs of the students, in both their instructional and their disciplinary functions, the anger and the alienation that lie behind adolescent violence will recede from the foreground of public education.

---

[27] Thomas A. Shaheen, quoted in report on seminar held in Columbus, May 15-16, 1969, "Principals Tackle Student Activism at SMI (School Management Institute) Seminar," *Ohio Schools* (Journal of Ohio Association of Secondary School Principals), May 23, 1969, p. 20.

[28] *American Teacher*, June 1969, p. 8.

[29] "Nothing Administrators Can Do Is Right," *I/D/E/A Reporter*, Spring Quarter 1969, p. 8.

FUTURE OF U.S. DEFENSE ECONOMY

by

Park Teter

PRESSURE TO PUT CURBS ON THE MILITARY
Revolt Against Military-Industrial Complex
Troop Withdrawal and Demobilization Planning
Intensification of Demand for Arms Limitation
Cries to Stop War and Tackle Social Problems

ECONOMIC ASPECTS OF MILITARY SPENDING
Effects of Cutbacks After Big and Small Wars
Differences Between Earlier Wars and Viet Nam
Regional Impact of Current Defense Spending

MEANS OF ADJUSTING TO REDUCED SPENDING
Availability of Various Tools to Sustain Demand
Reemployment of Defense Workers and Veterans
Programs to Assist Workers in Transition Period
Programs to Help Defense-Dependent Communities
Conversion Problems of the Defense Contractors

1 9 6 9
Sept. 24

FUTURE OF U. S. DEFENSE ECONOMY

DEFENSE SPENDING has been subjected in 1969 to more searching criticism than at any time since the cold war began. Attacks on the "military-industrial complex" in Congress and the press destroyed the nearly sacrosanct status formerly enjoyed by Defense Department budget requests. Although the critics failed to make any major dents in the military budget, the challenge they mounted was strong enough to put the Pentagon and its spokesmen in Congress on the defensive—a feat that would hardly have been possible a short while ago.

The outburst against military-industrial predominance coincided with four other developments pointing toward cutbacks in production for national defense: (1) The peace talks at Paris and initial troop withdrawals from Viet Nam focused attention on the economic consequences of bringing the war to an end; (2) plans for a multi-billion-dollar anti-ballistic missile system and other high-priced weapons sharpened interest in getting U. S.-Soviet talks on strategic arms limitation under way; (3) rising pressure for domestic programs to deal with the crisis in the cities established serious competition for dollars now spent on defense; and (4) inflation impelled the Nixon administration to effect certain cuts in the military budget. This multiple threat confronted defense industries, their employees, and their communities with the prospect of major dislocations in the foreseeable, if not the immediate, future.

REVOLT AGAINST MILITARY-INDUSTRIAL COMPLEX

When the Senate on Aug. 6 accepted development of the Safeguard A.B.M. system by a hairbreadth 51-50 vote, it was clear that the cold war tradition of congressional acquiescence in defense budgets was dead. The next day the Senate voted 47-46 to require quarterly Pentagon reports on all major weapons systems contracts and General Accounting Office audits and reports on such contracts. The military

107

procurement authorization bill was soon subjected to a blitz
of proposed reductions.

Attacks on the A.B.M. were only one reflection of growing
disenchantment with the defense establishment.[1] Supervision
of military spending had been growing into a major issue
as mounting public impatience with high taxes and inflation
gave new weight to familiar charges of waste and war-
profiteering in defense procurement. Such charges gained
wide publicity during hearings in November 1968 and January 1969 before the Subcommittee on Economy of the Joint
Economic Committee. In a report on May 27, 1969, the subcommittee, chaired by Sen. William Proxmire (D Wis.),
said Pentagon procurement practices resulted in "a vast
subsidy for the defense industry, particularly the larger
contractors, and in a greatly inflated defense budget."

The *cause célèbre* of the hearings was the disclosure that
the cost of the Lockheed Aircraft Corp.'s giant C-5A transport plane would run between $1.5 billion and $2 billion
over the original contract estimate. The House and Senate
Armed Services Committees held further hearings on the
C-5A in May and June, and during September the aircraft
was the key item in Senate debate on a $20 billion military
procurement authorization. When it came to a showdown,
Sept. 9, the Senate voted 64 to 23 against an amendment to
limit Air Force purchases of the C-5A to 58 planes. An even
larger majority, 75 to 7, voted Sept. 12 against an amendment to hold up construction of a $500 million nuclear air-
craft carrier. And four days later, on Sept. 16, the Senate
rejected 56-31 an amendment to slow down development of
a new strategic bomber to replace the B-52.[2]

Although the revolt against military spending thus made
no immediate headway in the Senate, and could not be expected to fare differently in the House, it unquestionably
represented a strong undercurrent of popular feeling that
has shown no sign of abating. Public frustration over the
Viet Nam war and its costs created a constituency for critics
of military spending that demonstrated its strength in a
Gallup poll reported Aug. 13, 1969. A majority of 52 per
cent of the participants expressing an opinion said the
United States was spending too much for national defense,

---

[1] See "Defense Criticism," *Congressional Quarterly Weekly Report*, March 28, 1969,
pp. 451-453.
[2] For an earlier controversy on a successor to the B-52, see "Defense Spending Management," *E.R.R.*, 1966 Vol. II, pp. 800-803.

31 per cent considered the rate of spending "about right," and 8 per cent favored increased defense expenditures.

The effect on the defense industry of the criticism in Congress and of public restlessness over military spending cannot be measured. But a recent article in *Fortune* magazine blamed "the changed political atmosphere" for the censure of the C-5A's cost and for hasty cancellation of an $875 million Lockheed contract for the Cheyenne helicopter.[3] The Defense Department's director of research and engineering, John S. Foster, conceded Aug. 19 that "Our past and present methods of acquiring weapons have lost us the confidence of the public." Foster warned that "the critical attitude toward the Defense Department may result in an actual reduction of the American effort" at a time when the Soviet Union is increasing military research and development.

TROOP WITHDRAWAL AND DEMOBILIZATION PLANNING

Although the Viet Nam peace talks drag on without apparent progress, pressure on the Nixon administration for a settlement and for large-scale U.S. troop withdrawals has not let up. Twenty-five thousand troops have already been pulled out, and an additional 35,000 are to be withdrawn by Dec. 15, 1969. On that date, however, the number of American troops remaining in Viet Nam may be as high as 484,000.

At the end of 1968 a special Cabinet committee submitted a report to President Johnson on economic planning for the period following the end of Viet Nam hostilities. The demobilization scenario on which the committee based its recommendations assumed full troop withdrawals would begin six months after a truce. In the following 12 months, total U.S. military personnel, at home and abroad, would be reduced by 800,000 and Defense Department civilian employees by 170,000 to produce an annual saving of $7 billion. Other operating expenditures would decline by $4 billion over a slightly longer period. After two and one-half years, military procurement would drop $8 billion below the level of spending required if the war were to continue.[4]

---

[3] Harold B. Meyers, "For Lockheed, Everything's Coming Up Unk-Unks," one of five articles on the defense industry in *Fortune*, Aug. 1, 1969.

[4] The committee's report was included in *Economic Report of the President* (January 1969), pp. 181-211. The total annual saving, two and one-half years after the truce, would fall $10 billion short of the estimated $29 billion a year being spent on the Viet Nam war. The difference arises from expected pay raises, price increases and program changes.

The President's 1969 Manpower Report estimated that about 900,000 of the 1.5 million civilians employed in defense-related jobs attributable to Viet Nam would be forced to seek new jobs. At the same time, reductions in the strength of the armed services would expand the civilian labor force. Most economists stress the importance of maintaining a high level of demand in the economy as a whole as the most crucial factor in adjustment to sharp reductions in demand for defense production and services. Expansionary fiscal and monetary policies, however, may be limited by the continuation of U. S. balance-of-payments difficulties and threats to the international stability of the dollar.

INTENSIFICATION OF DEMAND FOR ARMS LIMITATION

While an end to the Viet Nam war is not likely to hurt the highly specialized industries producing strategic weapons, another possibility on the horizon is aimed directly at them. Strategic arms limitation talks (SALT) between the United States and the Soviet Union are expected to be launched soon—possibly as early as mid-October 1969. Past disarmament negotiations have done little to slow the arms race, but a number of factors now intensify the pressures for agreement:

(1) The cost of strategic weapons, especially when added to the cost of the Viet Nam war, has generated public pressure, particularly among new voters, for an arms agreement that would permit diversion of spending to domestic priorities. While less subject to public pressures, the Soviet Government also feels the pinch of imbalance in its economic development.

(2) Development of spy satellites and other intelligence devices simplifies policing of any agreement and reduces the need for on-site inspections, which have been a major obstacle to agreement.

(3) Technological changes, particularly development of A.B.M. and M.I.R.V. (multiple independently targeted re-entry vehicle) systems, place both countries on the threshold of a new and very costly phase of arms competition.

(4) The nuclear non-proliferation treaty, approved in the Senate on March 13, 1969, by an 83-15 vote, provides a recent precedent for U. S.-Soviet recognition of common peril in the arms race.

(5) The threat of Russian-Chinese hostilities puts pressure on Soviet leaders to seek a détente with the West and eases Western fears of a monolithic Eurasian Communist bloc.

(6) The Soviet Union's achievement of approximate military parity with the United States might make it more amenable to halting or reducing some types of arms production.[5]

---

[5] The Institute for Strategic Studies in London reported in April: "The Soviet Union must now be treated as a full equal [of the United States] in terms both of strategic power and of her ability to control conflict in the developing world."— Quoted in *Fortune*, Aug. 1, 1969, p. 85.

Future of U. S. Defense Economy

President Nixon's election campaign demand for American superiority rather than parity in arms was clarified at a Jan. 27 news conference when he abandoned both terms in favor of "sufficiency."[6]

Despite the urgency of arms limitation, precedent is all on the side of the skeptics. The much less complex nuclear test ban treaty of 1963 and this year's non-proliferation treaty each required more than four years of strenuous negotiation. Defense industry officials look for uninterrupted competition with Soviet weapons development, and they are not alone. An unidentified high official of the U. S. Arms Control and Disarmament Agency was recently quoted as saying:

> We are now at the edge of a precipice where we can escalate sharply. The industry thinks that agreements to limit arms are unlikely and will go all out to realize their expectations. We are at the threshold of another round in the arms race, just as we were eight years ago when we went all out for long-range missiles.[7]

Whatever happens to strategic weapons development, the forces it has been thought necessary to maintain against the contingency of local wars are likely to fall below pre-Viet Nam levels. Popular hostility toward future Viet Nams has already prompted the Senate to record its view, in a 70-16 vote on June 26, 1969, that overseas commitments must not be made without congressional approval. The Pentagon's assumption that the United States should be prepared to wage simultaneous wars in Europe and Asia, plus a smaller conflict elsewhere, is now being reconsidered in a major study of U. S. military posture under the direction of Deputy Defense Secretary David Packard.

CRIES TO STOP WAR AND TACKLE SOCIAL PROBLEMS

Ever since riots in the ghettos began to dramatize domestic problems in the United States, pressures have been building for increased attention to civilian priorities. Inevitably, those concerned about fighting poverty, pollution, crime, and racial prejudice, and improving education, health, and the urban environment looked jealously at the largest drain on federal funds—the defense budget. President Johnson's policies gave a double impetus to a basic shift in attitudes toward military expenditures. On the one hand, his Great

---

[6] See "Prospects for Arms Control," *E.R.R.*, 1969 Vol. I, pp. 276-277.

[7] Bernard D. Nossiter, "Arms Firms See Postwar Spurt," *Washington Post*, Dec. 8, 1968.

Society programs inspired hopes of solving long-standing social problems. On the other hand, the Viet Nam war took away the funds required for these programs.

By both discrediting global military efforts and hobbling social action at home, the war has contributed more than anything else to the current outcry against defense spending. The younger generation, who scarcely recall the cold war atmosphere of the Berlin airlift, the Korean War, or the "missile gap" but who are liable to be drafted to fight against the Viet Cong, are in the vanguard of the campaign to spend dollars on the underprivileged rather than on weapons. Pressures against defense spending may be expected to increase as this generation becomes an increasingly large portion of the electorate. In the 1970 elections the number of persons "under thirty" eligible to vote will number 4.7 million more than in the last off-year election of 1966 and will comprise 22.4 per cent of the voting-age population.

A list of new programs or major expansions of existing federal programs, included for purposes of illustration in President Johnson's 1969 Economic Report, bore a total estimated price tag of $40 billion for fiscal 1972. Assuming peace in Viet Nam, the funds expected to be available by then from reduced defense outlays plus natural growth in tax revenues were estimated to total only $22 billion.

The Nixon administration expects a smaller "peace and growth dividend." The size of this dividend has been the subject of much debate; it cannot be estimated with any confidence until the current review of global strategy and military posture is completed. Postponement of strategic weapons development during the Viet Nam war and expansion of the Soviet navy have generated strong demand in the Pentagon for costly new weapons.

Whatever the size of the dividend, its distribution may be largely determined before it even appears. President Nixon's welfare program, submitted to Congress Aug. 11, 1969, would add an estimated $4 billion to federal welfare costs in its first full year of operation. The President's plan for sharing federal revenues with the states would, if approved, take a growing chunk of the federal budget that would climb to about $5 billion by fiscal 1976. And if tax reforms expected this year take the form of the bill passed by the House

Aug. 8, revenue losses will reach $4.1 billion in calendar 1972. Administration plans to reduce the national debt, in order to make credit more readily available for private construction, would also reduce the amount available for other domestic programs. Another domestic priority—combating inflation—has already prompted the administration to cut $3 billion from the proposed fiscal 1970 defense budget.

Because projects for which the politicians and the public are impatient add up to so much more than peacetime budgets can finance, competition among them is certain to intensify jealousy of enormous defense expenditures. The domestic programs now under consideration could add to those ongoing obligations of the federal government which are extremely difficult to reduce and which have, in fact, a natural proclivity for expansion. The eventual result might be to reverse the present balance between defense and civilian spending, in which domestic programs have to fight for the scraps left by the military.

Economic Aspects of Military Spending

AS PRESIDENT Eisenhower observed in his farewell address, a permanent arms industry of vast proportions joined to an immense military establishment is "something new in the American experience." The way in which the economy adjusts, or fails to adjust, to major shifts in the defense industry will influence the course of the nation's adaptation to permanently threatened national security.

Despite the newness of its situation, the United States has had some experience with modern demobilization. There are lessons to be gained from those experiences, but there are also changes in the structure of the defense industry since the last major reduction in defense spending at the end of the Korean War.

EFFECTS OF CUTBACKS AFTER BIG AND SMALL WARS

During World War II there was grave concern that massive demobilization at the end of the war would plunge the nation back into the depression conditions of the 1930s. In the nine months following the war, almost eight million men were released from military service. An additional four million defense workers were laid off, thus freeing a total of 12 million or about one-fourth of the nation's work force. The postwar decline in defense spending was equivalent to one-third of the gross national product, an awesome amount when one considers that total defense spending now amounts to less than 10 per cent of the current G.N.P. And yet unemployment in the demobilization period after World War II never rose above 4 per cent.

The great success of the demobilization derived from high aggregate demand in the civilian sector. Postponed needs and pent-up consumer demand, accumulated during the war, kept the economy in high gear. The government helped the transition through tax reduction, veterans' benefits, rapid property disposal and contract terminations, and easy credit policies.

Though much smaller, the post-Korea demobilization caused a mild recession. Defense spending fell from $50.4 billion in fiscal 1953 to $40.7 billion in fiscal 1954, contributing to a rise in unemployment to 5.6 per cent of the labor force in 1954. Although tax cuts supported disposable income and consumption, economists feel that more vigorous fiscal and monetary policies would have eased the transition.[8]

Since the Korean War, other shifts in defense production have not caused severe dislocation. For example, a drop in spending for tanks, conventional ordnance and commercial types of hard goods from $11 billion in fiscal 1953 to about $2 billion in fiscal 1957 constituted a huge loss of defense business for the Midwest. But because the production and manpower resources involved were not highly specialized, they were readily diffused into a civilian economy sustained by high demand. During a leveling of defense spending in 1963-64, the national unemployment rate actually fell.

DIFFERENCES BETWEEN EARLIER WARS AND VIET NAM

Changes since the Korean War would affect the character of any adjustment to defense cutbacks today. In 1965 a special Presidential committee observed that earlier demobilizations largely entailed reconversion—a return to production of previously produced goods. Many of the manufacturers had assumed that defense work would be a temporary diver-

---

[8] See "Arms Cutbacks and Economic Dislocation," *E.R.R.*, 1964 Vol. I, p. 121.

sion. At present, numerous companies have never produced to any significant degree for non-military markets.[9]

This specialization is particularly evident in the highly scientific aerospace industry, which expanded rapidly following the Soviet Union's successful launching of its first satellite in 1957. However, during the Viet Nam war the aerospace industry's share of federal defense and space expenditures has fallen from a high of 30.7 per cent in fiscal 1964 to an estimated 25.7 per cent for fiscal 1970.[10]

The buildup for Viet Nam had its greatest impact on employment in the aircraft, ordnance and communications industries. In fiscal 1967, the latest for which figures are available, the jobs of about 100,000 additional workers in the ordnance industry were attributable to Viet Nam, and they accounted for 50 per cent of the employment in the industry generated by the Defense Department and to 37 per cent of total employment in the industry. The war added about 140,000 workers in the aircraft industry, and they constituted 30 per cent of defense-generated employment and 17.5 per cent of total employment in the industry. Around 50,000 additional workers in communications equipment production made up 22 per cent of the industry's defense-generated employment and about 7.5 per cent of its total employment.

In a number of industries large increases in employment due to Viet Nam constituted only a small portion of the total work force. For example, nearly two-thirds of defense-generated employment in clothing manufacture was derived from the buildup, but the more than 30,000 added workers made up only 2 per cent of total employment in the industry. Similar trends were evident in the manufacture of steel and nonferrous metals, chemicals and textiles.[11]

The spread of war production among industries with large civilian markets makes the current defense budget more like those of the Korean War and less like recent cold war emphasis on strategic weapons development and production. As a result, economist Murray L. Weidenbaum (now an Assistant Secretary of the Treasury) said two years ago:

---

[9] *Report of the Committee on the Economic Impact of Defense and Disarmament* (July 1965), p. 11.
[10] *1969 Aerospace Facts and Figures* (Aerospace Industries Assn.).
[11] Richard P. Oliver, "The Employment Effect of Defense Expenditures," *Monthly Labor Review*, September 1967, pp. 9-16. Slight revisions of figures given in the article are based on subsequent refinement of data by the Bureau of Labor Statistics. Updated figures are to be published in the December 1969 issue of the *Review*.

"Much of the expansion in Viet Nam requirements has been met by production of civilian-oriented industries which should experience relatively minor difficulties if aggregate demand is maintained in the economy as a whole. The companies and the localities which are most directly dependent on defense work might actually gain from a reorientation of the military budget away from conventional equipment and towards high technology products and services." [12]

REGIONAL IMPACT OF CURRENT DEFENSE SPENDING

The Viet Nam war has shifted somewhat the regional distribution of defense spending. The combined share of the three Pacific Coast states, while still larger than that of any other region, dropped from 24.7 per cent of the total dollar value of military prime contracts in fiscal 1965 to 19.1 per cent in fiscal 1968. The share of the South Central states in the same period rose from 10.4 to 16.7 per cent.

No other region shifted as much as two percentage points, but individual states experienced dramatic changes. Alabama, Connecticut, Illinois, Minnesota, Mississippi, Tennessee, Texas and Wisconsin in fiscal 1968 more than doubled their pre-war share of the dollar value of prime contracts. A few states experienced sharp reductions. Washington, for example, received $530 million in defense contracts in 1968, compared to $1.1 billion in fiscal 1964. Colorado in the same period dropped from $390 million to $263 million. [13]

Nine states in fiscal 1968 had over $200 in prime military contracts per inhabitant—California, Connecticut, Georgia, Indiana, Massachusetts, Missouri, New Hampshire, Texas and Vermont. It is often asserted that subcontracting spreads the spending more widely among the states, but a recent analysis of a sample of subcontracting employment figures cast some doubt on that hypothesis. [14]

Between June 1965 and June 1968 no state declined in employment attributable to defense. As one would expect, the largest absolute increases in defense-generated employment in this period occurred in more populous states—California (137,100), Texas (82,700), Pennsylvania (48,600)

12 Murray L. Weidenbaum, *Peace in Vietnam: Possible Economic Impacts and the Business Response* (unpublished report prepared for the Committee on the Economic Impact of Peace in Vietnam, Chamber of Commerce of the United States, September 1967), p. 19.
13 Murray L. Weidenbaum, "After Vietnam, Our Vietnamized Economy," *Saturday Review*, May 24, 1969.
14 Roger F. Riefler and Paul B. Downing, "Regional Effect of Defense Effort on Employment," *Monthly Labor Review*, July 1968, pp. 1, 6.

IMPACT OF DEFENSE SPENDING, BY STATES, 1965-1968

| | Defense-generated employment (thousands) | | Defense dependency ratio as % of labor force | Military prime contracts fiscal '68 |
	June '65	June '68	June '67	(millions)
Alabama	47.5	59.1	4.2	$ 409.2
Alaska	8.8	10.2	9.8	106.5
Arizona	14.9	26.1	4.2	287.1
Arkansas	5.6	11.5	1.7	121.3
California	354.4	491.5	6.5	6,471.9
Colorado	24.1	30.8	3.4	262.8
Connecticut	68.0	116.3	7.5	2,355.1
Delaware	2.0	2.8	1.3	42.6
District of Columbia	33.2	43.1	10.3	349.8
Florida	68.5	94.9	3.5	975.8
Georgia	58.4	77.2	4.8	964.2
Hawaii	20.8	27.7	8.8	95.6
Idaho	0.6	1.2	0.4	17.1
Illinois	48.7	83.3	1.8	932.1
Indiana	35.3	72.3	3.1	1,107.5
Iowa	7.9	13.8	1.2	261.0
Kansas	19.4	22.8	3.3	292.3
Kentucky	13.3	19.6	1.9	60.4
Louisiana	10.6	17.9	1.7	460.5
Maine	5.6	8.4	1.9	75.2
Maryland	70.7	87.5	6.9	703.5
Massachusetts	75.9	115.8	4.3	1,618.7
Michigan	30.3	39.3	1.4	796.3
Minnesota	17.3	34.6	2.2	620.3
Mississippi	23.3	38.0	3.1	369.2
Missouri	53.6	80.3	4.5	1,356.9
Montana	1.5	5.0	2.7	20.5
Nebraska	5.1	9.9	1.4	120.4
Nevada	3.0	3.3	1.6	17.9
New Hampshire	11.9	18.0	6.4	156.0
New Jersey	66.9	88.8	3.3	1,108.4
New Mexico	15.3	16.4	4.5	87.2
New York	132.2	168.4	2.1	3,483.7
North Carolina	26.0	44.3	2.0	487.3
North Dakota	2.7	5.6	1.3	68.1
Ohio	81.7	108.7	2.5	1,640.5
Oklahoma	31.0	43.6	4.4	164.9
Oregon	5.5	8.7	1.0	119.7
Pennsylvania	108.4	157.0	3.2	1,727.3
Rhode Island	13.4	17.1	5.3	126.4
South Carolina	19.2	28.0	3.0	133.0
South Dakota	2.1	2.7	0.7	33.6
Tennessee	25.0	45.8	2.8	541.6
Texas	118.1	200.8	4.3	4,087.2
Utah	28.7	36.2	9.9	131.2
Vermont	2.0	3.9	2.1	105.0
Virginia	112.6	149.7	8.4	692.7
Washington	45.7	54.5	4.3	529.6
West Virginia	4.9	8.6	1.5	132.0
Wisconsin	11.4	26.4	1.4	406.4
Wyoming	0.7	0.7	0.9	14.9
TOTAL	2,055.6	2,932.7	3.6	$37,248.1

and Connecticut (48,300). Excluding states with only very minor defense industry and installations, the sharpest *rate* of increase occurred in Indiana, Minnesota and Wisconsin, each of which at least doubled defense employment in the period.

These employment figures, compiled by the Economic Information System of the Defense Department and the National Aeronautics and Space Administration, reflected civilian employment in all military installations and in all prime contracts exceeding $10,000, but covered only the subcontracting reported by about 450 plants. The multiplier effect of defense employment on other production and services was not measured. The figures used indicated that defense employment absorbed more than 6 per cent of the work force in June 1967 in Alaska, California, Connecticut, the District of Columbia, Hawaii, Maryland, New Hampshire, Utah, and Virginia. The national average was 3.6 per cent.[15]

Means of Adjusting to Reduced Spending

CONFRONTED simultaneously by progressive withdrawal of American forces from Viet Nam, disarmament negotiations, attacks on the military-industrial complex, inflationary pressures on the defense budget, and a growing demand for domestic priorities, the defense industries face a troubled future. The fate of the companies engaged in defense production, of their employees, and of the communities in which they are situated will depend in large part on the adjustment of the national economy to reductions in military purchases. But even if the economy as a whole adjusts smoothly to defense cutbacks, there may be intense local difficulties. Advance planning for such difficulties is crucial to overcoming them.

AVAILABILITY OF VARIOUS TOOLS TO SUSTAIN DEMAND

The fiscal and monetary policies required to maintain aggregate demand during a decline in military demand will depend on the speed of demobilization and the trend of the economy at the time. In the scenario for Viet Nam peace outlined by President Johnson's special Cabinet committee

---

[15] See table on p. 721.

and included in the 1969 Economic Report, a shortfall of demand amounting to $18 billion, 18 months after a truce, was predicted in the absence of action to offset the drop in military expenditures.[16] Unless stabilizing action were taken, this gap could be multiplied by induced cutbacks in the private sector to reach $40 billion two years after the truce.

To maintain demand, the peace-and-growth dividend could be used either for increased government spending in civilian programs or for tax reductions that would stimulate private consumption. Some combination of these two approaches is generally expected. An end to the war-imposed income tax surcharge is a common feature of most projections, as is increased federal spending to reduce poverty and improve the urban environment.

Decisions on priorities among government programs and among tax cuts must depend in part on the pace of demobilization, because some policies stimulate demand more rapidly than others. Lead times in government programs, especially many federal grant programs to states and communities, delay their impact on purchases more than would be the case with tax reductions. Liberalization of such income-support programs as unemployment compensation or public assistance, and the acceleration of government expenditures already programed, are measures which would permit a more rapid stimulus than pursuit of new efforts. The 1969 Economic Report urged that a program of accelerated expenditures which could be instituted on short notice be available for the President's consideration. It estimated that such a program could add up to $3 billion to federal spending in six months, and up to $7.5 billion in 12 months. The report urged that any plans to be put into effect during a transition to peacetime spending be submitted to Congress soon for debate and perhaps for enactment on a standby basis.

Both government spending and tax cuts could be limited by the need for fiscal policies to combat inflation and improve the balance of international payments. Nixon administration officials have indicated that budget surpluses would be used after the Viet Nam war to reduce the national debt

---

[16] *Economic Report of the President* (January 1969), p. 195. Of the total shortfall, $16 billion would derive from reduced defense spending, and $2 billion would constitute the increment in demand needed to absorb the addition of 600,000 persons to the civilian labor force.

and thus make mortgage funds available at lower interest rates for private construction.

The Economic Report asserted that the basic choice between reducing taxes and increasing expenditures should not be governed by considerations of economic stabilization; various mixes of increased spending and reduced taxes would be equally satisfactory from that standpoint. The choice should depend, the report said, upon the extent to which the nation wishes to divert resources from defense uses into other areas of the public sector. It urged that priorities be set in advance.

Weidenbaum has warned that indecisiveness in monetary and fiscal responses to defense cutbacks, arising from hesitation in choosing among alternatives, might produce a needless recession. He has warned also that unemployment and fears of a major depression might result from inaction and in turn generate public pressure for large-scale government intervention and spending. "Were this to happen, the rapid expansion in the public sector brought about by the Viet Nam buildup might prove not to be temporary but to represent another long-term shift in the balance between public and private activities in the American economy." [17]

REEMPLOYMENT OF DEFENSE WORKERS AND VETERANS

In the rapid demobilization assumed in the Economic Report, there would be a net addition of 600,000 persons to the private labor force in the first 18 months after a Viet Nam truce. The decline in defense purchases would also require job shifts in the same period among as many as 750,000 additional workers. The two groups combined would be seeking an average of about 75,000 jobs per month above the normal rate. Because the monthly hiring rate in manufacturing alone averaged 730,000 in 1966 and 640,000 in 1967, the report regarded the post-Viet Nam employment needs as "significant—but not enormous."

A study, prepared for the U. S. Arms Control and Disarmament Agency, of the experiences of defense workers laid off at three aerospace defense plants, concluded that "The single most important reform of the labor market that would reduce appreciably the reemployment transition costs would be a sweeping overhaul of the [job] information channels." [18] The California Department of Employment, in

[18] *Reemployment Experiences of Defense Workers* (December 1968), p. iii.
[17] Murray L. Weidenbaum, *Peace in Vietnam: Possible Economic Impacts and the Business Response* (cited), p. 23.

a report likewise prepared for the Arms Control and Disarmament Agency, published information to facilitate job transfers from technical and skilled production occupations peculiar to the missile industry or so concentrated in that industry as to present transfer problems.[19] It found that most of the defense jobs it studied had counterparts in nondefense industries sufficiently similar in skills to permit transfer of workers with little or no additional training. Because missile production is among the most highly specialized defense industries, this finding augured well for reemployment in less sophisticated arms production. However, the California report noted that, even where skills were similar, in three out of four occupations surveyed the transfer to non-defense jobs was limited by at least one of the following factors: the demand for workers in the counterpart occupation, comparability of wages, union regulations, specific company hiring practices, and federal licensing requirements.

The California report emphasized the importance of the availability of information for reemployment; it specifically urged that the defense plant staff concerned with training or wages and salaries be fully utilized for its knowledge of similarities between defense and non-defense job requirements. The report proposed that defense contractors be required to classify all employee positions in accordance with the Dictionary of Occupational Titles in order to facilitate comparison of jobs from plant to plant.

PROGRAMS TO ASSIST WORKERS IN TRANSITION PERIOD

A number of federal programs already exist to aid workers caught in the transition to reduced defense efforts. Returning veterans receive particular attention from the federal-state Employment Service, and since 1967 special Veterans Assistance Centers have been established in 21 cities by the Veterans Administration. These centers place particular emphasis on the 25 per cent of veterans with less than a high school education. During their last six months in military service, men facing discharge without adequate work preparation are eligible for counseling, training, education and placement services provided at about 250 installations by a combination of private industry and federal, state and local agencies.

---

[19] California Department of Employment, *The Potential Transfer of Industrial Skills from Defense to Nondefense Industries* (April 1968), pp. 13-18.

The Department of Defense guarantees new job opportunities for career civilian employees dislocated by the closing of a military installation. The plan includes reimbursement for moving costs and protection of incomes during periods of transition. A computerized central referral unit in Dayton, Ohio, is used to match employees with vacancies. The program is not available to defense workers employed by private industry on government contracts.

Expansion of the federal-state Employment Service and training programs under the Manpower Development and Training Act would be required to handle increases in job seekers. The 1969 Economic Report recommended such expansion and also proposed a program of loans and grants for relocation assistance to low- and middle-income workers affected by cutbacks in specified defense-dependent communities. To prevent widespread loss of homes in areas suffering temporary unemployment, the report urged adoption of a program to encourage private lenders to defer mortgage payments on homes of persons dislocated by defense cutbacks. In the absence of such a moratorium, the report called for government loans to cover mortgage payments.

Whether or not unemployed defense workers should be singled out for more generous treatment than other unemployed persons has not been determined. The 1965 report of the President's Committee on the Economic Impact of Defense and Disarmament noted that a worker "bumped" by someone shifted from defense work, or a salesman laid off where retail trade had declined with defense production, was as deserving of assistance as an unemployed defense worker. The committee voiced doubt that relocation assistance would be justified except as part of a general program available to all.[20] Non-defense workers may well be the hardest hit. The 1969 Manpower Report observed that "A temporary rise in unemployment would intensify the job-seeking difficulties of disadvantaged workers with the flow into the labor market of educated, skilled and experienced workers competing for available jobs."[21]

The local adjustments to reductions in defense employment may have an important effect on the national economy.

---

[20] *Report of the Committee on the Economic Impact of Defense and Disarmament* (July 1965), p. 48.
[21] *Manpower Report of the President* (January 1969), p. 69.

Economist Leslie Fishman goes so far as to say that "micro" market adjustments may be decisive in maintaining employment because the balance-of-payments problem would inhibit fiscal policies that create demand in the national market. Fishman suggested that demobilization would offer an opportunity for "giant strides" in information channeling and employment decision theory that "could lead not only to smooth and successful transitions, but also to a new era in the operation of the labor markets." He asserted that "Improved operation of the labor market could easily reduce the unemployment rate to levels long familiar to the West German economy, increase efficiency and productivity, and thus become a strong force against inflation." [22]

PROGRAMS TO HELP DEFENSE-DEPENDENT COMMUNITIES

Although shifts in industrial production are a normal feature of the dynamic American economy, the volatile character of defense procurement makes communities which are heavily dependent on it subject to particularly severe dislocation.

The Defense Department's Office of Economic Adjustment since 1961 has sought to assist communities affected by closing of military installations. The office gives advice in analyzing a community's needs and assets and in planning for conversion and incorporation of obsolete installations into efforts organized by the community. It also provides liaison with federal agencies authorized to assist economic recovery. The office does not have legislative authority to assist communities affected by cutbacks in defense production by private industry.

However, a number of programs of civilian federal agencies are available to communities affected by major reductions in defense production. If unemployment suddenly rises to 50 per cent or more above the national average, or there is reason to expect it to reach that level, a community qualifies for assistance from the Economic Development Administration, established in the Commerce Department in 1965. Once the community has prepared an over-all economic development program, E.D.A. may provide any of the following: a) financial assistance for economic planning; b) technical assistance, research and informational aid; c) ad-

---

[22] Leslie Fishman, "Author's Note on Applicability to Economic Adjustment—Post Viet Nam and Disarmament," in *Reemployment Experiences of Defense Workers* (December 1968), pp. 230, 236.

vances for public works planning; d) plans to enable advance acquisition of land for public works; e) grants for public works; f) preferential treatment in disposal of surplus federal property; and g) loans to local development corporations.

Small Business Administration loans, Labor Department training programs, and grants to assist urban development planning also are available to communities adjusting to loss of defense activity. In communities affected by closing of government installations, the General Services Administration may ease the impact by arranging for use of the property by other federal agencies, by donating it for public purposes, or by selling it for industrial use.

Delay in implementing adjustment plans is likely to start a downward spiral in a community deprived of defense activity. As the work force scatters in search of jobs, it becomes more difficult to attract new enterprises. A consistent theme of studies of areas hit by defense cutbacks is the need for a local committee to develop in advance plans for community adjustment. Most studies stress that local initiative and responsibility are essential.

President Johnson's final Economic Report recommended establishment of a Readjustment Operations Committee for detailed planning of readjustment assistance and for coordination with state and local authorities. The proposed committee would also develop inventories of the skills of defense workers and military personnel for matching with the requirements of potential sources of employment in defense-dependent areas.

CONVERSION PROBLEMS OF THE DEFENSE CONTRACTORS

A corporation can cope with cuts in defense orders in three ways. It can sell or deactivate plant or equipment and continue to operate on a smaller scale while its manpower is diffused in the economy. It can diversify by developing or acquiring capacity to produce for civilian markets, in order to cushion the shock of defense cuts and pave the way for expansion in non-defense production. Or it can convert its entire productive capacity from swords to plowshares.

For many industries whose defense orders have expanded during the Viet Nam war, conversion would merely constitute a return to pre-war activities. To shift from production of items like uniforms and C-rations to civilian goods would require minimum adaptation. Companies for which military procurement provides only a small part of the total market, as in the case of automobile manufacturers, are sufficiently diversified to accommodate readily to defense cuts and shift resources to other activities.

A bill introduced in the House by Rep. F. Bradford Morse (R Mass.) and a companion bill in the Senate by Sen. George McGovern (D S.D.) would, in addition to creating a National Economic Conversion Commission, require all Defense Department and Atomic Energy Commission contractors to define their capability for converting their manpower and facilities from military to civilian uses.[23] The difficulties of such conversion were summarized in a recent study prepared for the U.S. Arms Control and Disarmament Agency by the University of Denver Research Institute:

> Unfortunately there is little evidence that defense firms can easily achieve rapid, profitable conversion. Defense industry is uniquely specialized. It is set up to develop and produce limited numbers of technically sophisticated, expensive systems. It is also organized to deal largely with a single, rich, hierarchically organized customer who participates actively in the management of each firm. Rapid conversion of defense industry resources appears feasible only when directed into fields with similar customer requirements and customer participation.[24]

Not all assessments have been so cautious. The very sophistication of such specialized industries as missile production tempts speculation on the benefits to be reaped by application of such concentrated talent to civilian problems. "The application of systems management techniques to a large variety of non-defense management and design problems holds great promise for the future," the 1965 report of the Economic Impact committee suggested.[25] The June 5, 1967, issue of *Technology Week* was devoted entirely to the market for aerospace capacities in federal agencies other than the Defense Department and NASA. It found prospective markets worth about $5 billion, including projects in fields as diverse as oceanology, high-speed ground transportation, and water pollution.

---

[23] The McGovern bill has a score of co-sponsors, and around 80 House members have introduced bills paralleling the Morse bill.

[24] University of Denver Research Institute, *Defense Systems Resources in the Civil Sector: An Evolving Approach, an Uncertain Market* (July 1967), p. 104.

[25] Report of the Committee on the Economic Impact of Defense and Disarmament (July 1965), p. 23.

In an effort to capitalize on aerospace talent and prepare for possible dislocation in the state's large defense industry, California in 1965 launched four experimental studies of civilian problems by defense contractors. Crime and delinquency, government information, urban mass transportation, and waste management were analyzed respectively by the Space-General Corp., Lockheed Missiles and Space Co., North American Aviation, and Aerojet-General Corp. The National Institute of Public Affairs, which reviewed the studies, concluded, in the words of Institute President Carl F. Stover, that "Without question, the California studies proved the feasibility of bringing industrially based capabilities in systems analysis, engineering, and management to bear productively in dealing with public problems outside the defense and space programs." [26]

However, Bernard D. Nossiter in a recent *Washington Post* review of post-Viet Nam plans of the aerospace companies reported that leaders of the industry were in agreement that the outcome of the California experiment was not happy. They were not prepared for some difficulties familiar to other businessmen, such as the fragmentation of local political authority, and they missed the indulgent patronage of the military, under whom they could afford to surround a problem with a myriad of scientists and engineers. However, Nossiter found "a nagging belief in the industry that it should widen its scope." He quoted James Ling, head of Ling-Temco-Vought, Inc., on one way of doing it: "I frankly don't see how we could tackle things like urban renewal or pollution. But we could buy a company to do it." [27]

One expert warned against the possible long-term consequences of expanding the civilian use of defense industry, "which increasingly develops the characteristics and mentality of a government arsenal" rather than "the risk-bearing and entrepreneurship which is characteristic of private enterprise." He also asked: "In encouraging these companies to expand into civilian government markets, are we in the process of setting up a civilian counterpart of what has been labeled, or perhaps mislabeled, a 'military-industrial complex'?" [28]

---

[26] "The California Experiment—an Appraisal," reprinted in University of Denver Research Institute, *op. cit.*, Appendix D, p. 160.

[27] Bernard D. Nossiter, "Defense Firms Leery of Civilian Work," *Washington Post*, Dec. 9, 1968.

[28] Murray L. Weidenbaum, "Arms and the American Economy: A Domestic Convergence Hypothesis," in the *American Economic Review*, May 1968, p. 436.

Mission to Mars: Benefits vs. Costs

by

Richard L. Worsnop

1 9 6 9
Oct. 1

MISSION TO MARS: BENEFITS VS. COSTS

PRESIDENT NIXON soon will decide whether the United States should adopt the goal of landing men on Mars before the end of the century. The President has before him a report by a special Space Task Group whose primary recommendation was that this country undertake such a mission. It is now up to Nixon to decide whether to accept one of the task group's suggested Mars landing dates—1983, 1986, or sometime in the 1990s—or to suspend judgment, at least for the time being. Whatever decision the President makes, it is sure to be preceded by vigorous debate among the public and in Congress.

The Space Task Group report, made public Sept. 17,[1] gave the President three "options" on a Mars manned landing. Under the option that would land men on Mars in 1983, the federal space budget would increase to $4.2 billion in fiscal 1971—up by $500 million from the fiscal 1970 budget request—to $4.8 billion in fiscal 1972, $6 billion in fiscal 1973, and almost $7 billion in fiscal 1974. The final decision whether to go ahead with the Mars landing would be made in 1974 if the foregoing timetable were adopted. A favorable decision would mean that the space budget would climb to $7.7 billion in fiscal 1975 and continue to increase over the following five years to a peak of $9.4 billion in fiscal 1980.

The option that Agnew favors—adoption of a 1986 Mars landing goal—would keep NASA spending below $5 billion a year until fiscal 1975, when it would reach $5.5 billion. Congress and the then-President would decide in 1978, under this timetable, whether to proceed with the Mars program. If they did so, the NASA budget would mount to $6.6 billion in fiscal 1979 and to $7.7 billion the following year. Peak annual expenditures of $8 billion a year would be required in the early 1980s. National Aeronautics and Space Admin-

[1] Members of the task group were Vice President Spiro T. Agnew, chairman; presidential science adviser Lee A. DuBridge; National Aeronautics and Space Administrator Thomas O. Paine; and Air Force Secretary Robert C. Seamans.

istrator Thomas O. Paine said on Sept. 17 that a Mars program "should be no more expensive than the program to go to the moon." The lunar program has cost about $24 billion to date. Other estimates place the total cost of a Mars program as high as $100 billion.

The Space Task Group asserted that "manned exploration of the planets is the most challenging and most comprehensive of the many long-range goals available to the nation at this time, with manned exploration of Mars as the next step toward this goal." It was emphasized, however, that "manned planetary exploration would be a goal, not an immediate program commitment," as was the case with the lunar landing program. The task group also recommended that this country's long-range space program "should include progressively more sophisticated missions to the near planets as well as multiple-planet flyby missions to the outer planets, taking advantage of the favorable relative positions of the outer planets in the late 1970s." It added that "Early missions to the asteroid belt [situated between Mars and Jupiter] and to the vicinity of a comet should be planned."

The task group report amounted to a victory for the Vice President, who said in interviews at Cape Kennedy on the day of the Apollo 11 launching, July 16, 1969, that "We should articulate a simple, ambitious optimistic goal of a manned flight to Mars by the end of this century." Three weeks later, on Aug. 6, NASA Administrator Paine told a National Press Club audience that a manned Mars flight in the early 1980s would be a "focus" for NASA's long-range plans. These would include, among other projects, nine more lunar landings.

VARIOUS RESERVATIONS ABOUT THE MARS PROPOSAL

The Mars mission has encountered considerable resistance in Congress and among scientists. Rep. George P. Miller (D Calif.), chairman of the House Science and Astronautics Committee, said on Aug. 11 that any decision on a Mars landing should be delayed for five or 10 years while new technology is developed and more experience is gained in space flight. Rep. William F. Ryan (D N.Y.) asserted two days later that "The achievement of the Apollo program cannot be allowed to become the rationale for automatically approving the next goals of NASA." Ryan urged Congress to determine "the relative importance of whatever space program we wish to develop as opposed to the unfulfilled human needs on earth."

A number of scientists have expressed similar reservations. Dr. Joshua Lederberg, a former member of the space science board of the National Academy of Sciences and the National Research Council, recently opposed a manned Mars flight on "purely scientific grounds." Lederberg explained: "There is nothing that a man can do on board a Mars mission that is not vastly outweighed by the cost of sheltering and feeding him en route. Once there, he would make it impossible not to contaminate the planet with his litter, and his return carries the risk of contaminating the earth with his baggage." [2] Bruce Murray, professor of planetary science at the California Institute of Technology and a member of a team checking findings of the recent unmanned Mariner 6 and 7 flights past Mars, said on Aug. 20 that a manned mission to the red planet in the 1980s would be a "stunt." Murray urged, instead, continued exploration of the moon and a series of unmanned probes of the planets into the 1980s. "If we do these things now, by the 1980s we will be ready to think about sending men to Mars," he said. "There's no hurry."

The public also has misgivings about a manned Mars flight. In a Gallup Poll published Aug. 6, only 39 per cent of the respondents favored such a flight, while 53 per cent were opposed. A Harris Survey of Aug. 25 produced similar results. Asked if it were worth $4 billion a year for the next 10 years "to explore the moon and other planets in outer space," 44 per cent of those polled said "yes" and 47 per cent said "no."

Because a Mars program would be extremely expensive, it has been suggested that the United States and the Soviet Union—and perhaps other countries—pool their resources in such an undertaking. Sir Bernard Lovell, a professor of radio astronomy and director of the Jodrell Bank experimental station in England, has written that "the success of Apollo . . . demands international collaboration" because "there are no longer technical or physiological reasons why man should not soon begin the program of development necessary to send human beings to Mars." Lovell believes that a 1980-85 Mars landing date is "more realistic than the 10-year scale for the moon landing was in 1961" and

---

[2] Column in *Washington Post*, Aug. 16, 1969.

that "The history of our age shows that neither the Soviet Union nor America is likely to be deterred by cost when such a technical possibility occurs." [3]

TECHNICAL COMPLEXITIES OF EXPEDITION TO MARS

A round trip to Mars would be vastly more difficult than journeying to the moon and back. A major problem is distance. While orbiting around earth, the moon remains at a relatively fixed distance—between 221,000 and 252,000 miles —from the planet. But the distance between Mars and earth varies greatly, principally because each planet moves in a different orbit around the sun. The closest approaches of Mars to earth occur when the two planets are in opposition —that is, when they are so aligned that a straight line would pass from the sun through earth and through Mars, in that order. Since Mars takes almost twice as long—687 days—to orbit the sun as does earth, the planets are in opposition only once every two years and seven weeks. Moreover, "Because the eccentricity of the orbit of Mars is significantly greater than that of earth's orbit, the distance between the two planets varies from one opposition to the next. . . . The distance . . . ranges from somewhat less than 56 million kilometers (35 million miles) at the most favorable opposition to a little over 101 million kilometers (63 million miles) at the least favorable." [4] Mars will make an unusually close approach to earth—34.9 million miles—on Aug. 12, 1971. This is virtually the shortest distance between the two planets that is ever attained.

The distance between Mars and earth at opposition gives little indication, however, of the distance a space ship must travel from one planet to the other. Since Mars is a moving target, Mariner 6 logged 226 million miles and Mariner 7 logged 193 million miles before they passed by the red planet. Calculating the proper trajectory in such a situation is extremely difficult. John A. Stallkamp, a Mariner project scientist with NASA, likens the task to "leaving New York in a boat, making a last course-setting maneuver while still in sight of New York, then setting the rudder and hoping to make a harbor in England." Stallkamp points out that "You have both to aim for your target and take account of deflecting influences such as winds in that final maneuver." [5]

[3] Bernard Lovell, "Man Moves Into the Universe," *Bulletin of the Atomic Scientists*, September 1969, pp. 5-6.
[4] Samuel Glasstone, *The Book of Mars* (1968), p. 38.
[5] Quoted in *Christian Science Monitor*, Feb. 12, 1969.

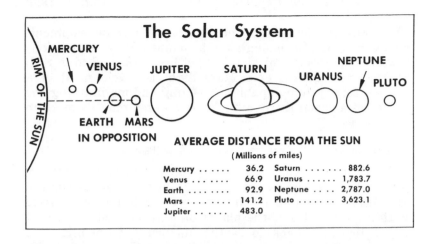

The Solar System

AVERAGE DISTANCE FROM THE SUN
(Millions of miles)

Mercury	36.2	Saturn	882.6
Venus	66.9	Uranus	1,783.7
Earth	92.9	Neptune	2,787.0
Mars	141.2	Pluto	3,623.1
Jupiter	483.0		

NASA Administrator Paine, in his Aug. 6 address, outlined the method by which the space agency envisions sending men to Mars.

We would plan to assemble two Mars vehicles with a six-man crew each in earth orbit. Each would probably be propelled by three nuclear rocket stages, side by side. The one in the middle would not be fired for the trip out to Mars, but would be used to come home. The two outer rockets would be fired to give the entire assembly the velocity required to fly out to the planet, after which they would peel off, retrofire, and return to earth.

Each Mars vehicle would then consist of the remaining nuclear rocket and a large life-support and work capsule, based on our space station design, together with Mars landing modules. The two spacecraft would journey out to Mars linked together into one ship, but would go into orbit around Mars separately by retrofiring their nuclear rockets. They would remain there for some 90 days, allowing half of each crew to descend to the surface and carry out surface experiments for about a month, after which they would return to orbit, and the ships would refire their nuclear rockets for the return to earth. . . . This space odyssey will require just under two years from the time that the astronauts leave earth orbit until they return.

Much preliminary work must be done before a manned Mars flight can be attempted. Projects deemed essential by NASA include development of (1) a 12-man orbiting space station; (2) a shuttle "bus" that can carry men to and from the station; (3) a space "tugboat" to push space stations together; (4) a nuclear engine to supply the rocket thrust needed for long excursions into space. Development of all this equipment was recommended in the task group's report.

The NERVA nuclear rocket engine, now under development, would be powerful enough for a manned Mars expedition; however, no specific mission has yet been assigned to it. Still another prerequisite of a Mars flight is development of a life-support system capable of feeding and maintaining the health of a dozen astronauts for two dozen months or so in outer space.

SIFTING OF DATA TRANSMITTED BY MARINER PROBES

Three unmanned American spacecraft already have explored Mars to the extent of taking pictures of its surface and measurements of its thin atmosphere. Mariner 4 passed within 6,118 miles of the planet on July 14, 1965, and sent 22 photographs back to earth; Mariner 6 transmitted 74 pictures from as close as 2,000 miles from Mars on July 29-30, 1969; and Mariner 7 radioed 126 pictures of the Martian surface to earth from as close as 2,200 miles from Mars on Aug. 5, 1969.

The photographs and other data sent back by the three Mariners show Mars to be more like the moon than like earth. For one thing, the Martian surface is heavily cratered, as is the lunar surface. A possibly important difference, however, is the fact that some of the craters on Mars appeared in photographs to be smooth and eroded—like "salad bowls." The reason for the apparent erosion is not known.

Much of the information relayed by the Mariners has raised more questions than it has answered. For example, astronomers on earth have long been puzzled by a W-shaped cloud that seems to hover fitfully over the Martian equator. In pictures transmitted by Mariners 6 and 7, the cloud showed up as three or more distinct white spots. These spots, it is now speculated, may be associated with a hot-spring area on the planet.

Data transmitted by various instruments aboard the Mariners indicate that the Martian environment is extremely harsh. Air pressure on the planet's surface, it was found, is so thin that it would be equivalent only to that at altitudes of 100,000 to 150,000 feet above earth. The ice formations at the southern polar cap of Mars have been tentatively identified as dry (carbon dioxide) rather than water ice. And the amount of ultraviolet solar radiation bombarding the

Mission to Mars: Benefits Vs. Costs

Martian surface is high enough to be lethal to virtually all forms of terrestrial life.

POSSIBILITIES OF FINDING LIFE ON THE RED PLANET

Despite the foregoing findings, the possibility that some living organisms might have evolved on Mars has not been ruled out. An infrared spectrometer on board Mariner 7 was thought to have detected two gases—ammonia and methane —that could indicate the presence of primitive life. Both are produced naturally on earth principally by biological decay. George C. Pimentel, a University of California chemist, said on Aug. 7 that the apparent traces of ammonia and methane in the Martian atmosphere might have been produced by such non-biological processes as "outgassing" from the planet's interior. On the other hand, he added, "One cannot restrain the speculation that the gases might be of biological origin." If so, he theorized, they might have been generated by organisms that found shelter in a relatively hospitable region near the edge of Mars' southern polar cap, where small but life-sustaining amounts of water ice might be available. Pimentel further speculated that clouds of carbon dioxide vapor over the south polar region might serve to shield the area from excessive ultraviolet radiation. Pimentel has since disowned his initial conclusions. Subsequent analysis of Mariner 6 and 7 data, Pimentel reported on Sept. 12, showed that what was thought to be ammonia and methane actually was carbon dioxide.

Laboratory experiments have nevertheless demonstrated that certain terrestrial organisms can live in a simulated Martian environment. Primitive forms of life are remarkably adaptable: Micro-organisms are found near the top of Mount Everest, and others thrive in hot springs where the temperature is near the boiling point of water. Moreover, some organisms can withstand great changes in temperature. Bacteria isolated from the hot soil around the volcano Mount Stromboli in Italy continued to grow in the simulated cold of a Martian environment.

It is of interest that terrestrial organisms, which normally live at very low temperatures in the polar regions, have evolved in such a manner that the water they contain does not freeze at 0° C (32° F), the normal freezing point. These organisms contain either dissolved salts, as in the halophilic bacteria, or an organic compound, such as a glycerol derivative, found in some insects, which acts as an "antifreeze." These solutes lower the freezing point of water to a temperature which is below that of the surroundings. Consequently, the water in the organism does not freeze even though the temperature falls below 0° C (32° F). Life forms with similar characteristics could have developed on Mars and would be well adapted to an environment in which the temperature fell below the normal freezing point of water every night.[6]

The thin atmosphere of Mars appears to consist primarily of carbon dioxide, with small amounts of water vapor and carbon monoxide present also. The amount of free oxygen in the Martian atmosphere probably would be too small to be of biological significance. Nevertheless, anaerobes— organisms capable of living in the absence of free oxygen— could survive in such an environment. There are a number of types of anaerobic bacteria on earth. They derive their energy from the oxidation of carbon and hydrogen in organic materials; but the oxidizing agent is not gaseous oxygen. It can be, among other things, a sulfate, a nitrate, nitrogen gas, or carbon dioxide. In the latter two cases, the products of oxidation are ammonia and methane, respectively.

Ultraviolet radiation and the scarcity, if not absence, of water are the two greatest impediments to the existence of life on Mars. Neither condition, however, necessarily forecloses the possibility of finding life there. Tests made with terrestrial organisms show that most are killed in a short time when exposed to ultraviolet radiation of the intensity expected on Mars. But the spores of some fungi, especially those having a red or black pigment, appear to be exceptionally resistant to ultraviolet rays. Furthermore, "soil is a very good absorber of ultraviolet radiation and, if they did not have to depend on photosynthesis to provide energy and nutriment, organisms on Mars could live a short distance below the soil and be completely protected." [7] And it is possible also that Martian organisms have developed some form of natural defense, such as a protective silica shell, against heavy radiation.

Because of the low pressure of water vapor in the Martian atmosphere, bodies of liquid water could not exist for an appreciable time even when the surface temperature was above the normal freezing point. Solidified water, in the form of hoarfrost, would tend to vaporize rather than to melt when the ground and atmosphere of Mars warm up in

---

[6] Samuel Glasstone, *op. cit.*, pp. 212-213.
[7] *Ibid.*, p. 216.

the spring. It has been suggested that there may be places on Mars where heat from the interior of the planet reaches the surface. The permafrost layer in these regions (if it exists) would melt and form water. As a result, there would be moist soil or possibly even a pond or small lake, continuously fed by the melting frost.

Norman H. Horowitz, a professor of biology at the California Institute of Technology and a specialist in extraterrestrial life, has stated that "It is certainly true that no terrestrial species could survive under average Martian conditions . . . except in the dormant state." However, Horowitz adds that "If we admit the possibility that Mars once had a more favorable climate which was gradually transformed to the severe one . . . [of] today, and if we accept the possibility that life arose on the planet during this earlier epoch, then we cannot exclude the possibility that Martian life succeeded in adapting itself to the changing conditions and remains there still." [8]

Two days after Mariner 7 passed by Mars, Horowitz said he had "never considered the probability of finding life on Mars is very high." However, he went on to say that "discovery of life on another planet would be of transcendent importance," and even a remote possibility of its existing on Mars would be justification for searching for it. On Sept. 11, after further analysis of the Mariner data, Horowitz concluded that "There is nothing . . . that encourages the belief that Mars is an abode of life." He added that if life "does exist, it's microbial," but that its existence cannot be ruled out until a projected Mars landing laboratory is placed on the surface of the planet.

INTEREST OF NASA IN FUTURE OF SPACE PROGRAM

A national commitment to land men on Mars, or adoption of an alternative manned space flight program, is deemed essential by NASA. Space agency officials calculate that two or three manned flights a year are needed to keep this country's facilities at Cape Kennedy and Houston, and its worldwide network of tracking stations, in working order. Any lesser effort, they say, would produce stagnation and thus waste of the billions of dollars invested in the entire space program to date.

NASA already is feeling the post-Apollo pinch. Wernher

---

[8] Quoted by Samuel Glasstone, *op. cit.*, p. 217.

von Braun, director of the Marshall Space Flight Center, Huntsville, Ala., pointed out last October that the Apollo program at its peak employed 300,000 persons throughout the aerospace industry. By the end of 1969, however, "We will be down from our original 300,000 to 162,000 for that program." Von Braun said that "Where the thing really begins to hurt is when the engineers, the scientists and the special skills—when they are laid off also, because you just dissipate the capability that you have built up, and as a result you are depriving yourself of the real payoff of your initial investment." [9]

The doldrums into which NASA has drifted is reflected in the recent market performance of aerospace stocks. North American Rockwell, the leading Apollo program contractor, saw its common stock drop in value from a 1968 high of 44⅞ to 27 on Sept. 24, 1969. Wall Street analysts are pessimistic about the future of aerospace industries. Much of the bearish outlook stems from realization that work on Apollo has, in effect, been completed. Although nine more manned missions to the moon are planned by NASA, command and service modules for six of the missions already are in the final assembly stage at North American Rockwell.

Science magazine recently pointed out that "To the plans for the Mars venture, the verdict is less likely to be Yes than Maybe, but NASA expects this." On the other hand, "If the pace of development . . . is not quite so brisk as [NASA] would like, the agency knows that Mars will still be out there." [10]

Slow Growth of Knowledge About Mars

MARS always has held special fascination for man because of its proximity [11] and its distinctive reddish color, suggestive of blood and fire. To the Sumerians and other early civilizations, the planet became a symbol of the carnage and destruction of war. The Chaldeans, about 3,000 years ago, named it Nergal for the master of battles. Later, the Greeks

---

[9] Interview in *U. S. News & World Report*, Oct. 14, 1968, p. 75.

[10] "Post-Apollo: NASA Seeks a Mars Flight Plan," *Science*, Sept. 5, 1969, p. 991.

[11] Venus comes closer to earth than does Mars, but at the time when it is nearest the illuminated hemisphere is turned away from earth and consequently cannot be seen.

referred to the red planet as Ares, for their god of war, and the Romans christened it Mars. In the course of time, the red planet came to be called Mars (or its equivalent) in most languages.[12]

EVOLUTION OF THEORIES ABOUT THE SOLAR SYSTEM

Some of the most important early discoveries about the solar system stemmed from observation of Mars. The Greek scholar Aristarchus of Samos, who lived in the third century B.C., is said to have suggested that earth and the planets might be revolving about the sun. But this view found little support because of the strongly entrenched opinion among the Greeks that earth was the fixed center of the universe.

The earth-centric theory found its most persuasive expression in the writings of Claudius Ptolemaeus (Ptolemy), a Greco-Egyptian who lived in Alexandria in the second century A.D. According to Ptolemy, earth was stationary and around it revolved the seven planets known at the time in the following order: The moon, Mercury, Venus, the sun, Mars, Jupiter, and Saturn. The planets were supposed to move in a series of circles with earth at the center. So convincing was Ptolemy that his system of planetary motion remained virtually unchallenged for more than 1,400 years.

The first great challenge came in 1543 with publication of the Polish astronomer Nicholas Copernicus' great work *On the Revolutions of the Celestial Bodies.* In the Copernican system, the sun was stationary and the planets, including earth but not the moon, revolved around it. Although Copernicus essentially was correct, his theories failed at first to dislodge the Ptolemaic system. It fell to the German astronomer Johannes Kepler to refine the Copernican thesis. On the basis of his observations and those of the Danish astronomer Tycho Brahe, Kepler formulated his three laws of planetary motion, the first two of which stemmed from study of the orbit of Mars. Kepler's first law holds that the orbit of each planet is an ellipse instead of a circle. Actually, planetary orbits around the sun do not deviate greatly from circles. The orbit of Mars, however, differs appreciably from the circular, as can be seen in the differing distances between Mars and earth when the two planets are in opposition.

---

[12] A reminder of the seven planets of the ancients may be found in the names of the days of the week: Sunday (sun); Monday (moon); Tuesday (French, *mardi*, Mars); Wednesday (*mercredi*, Mercury); Thursday (*jeudi*, Jove or Jupiter); Friday (*vendredi*, Venus); Saturday (Saturn).

Invention of the telescope in 1608 provided additional support for the Copernican system and also afforded more detailed visual examination of Mars. Galileo Galilei observed as early as 1610 that Mars was "not perfectly round." The first recognizable drawing of the planet was made in 1659 by Christian Huygens, a Dutch mathematician and physicist. Huygens was able to show that Mars rotates, like earth, about a north-south axis, and that the period of rotation— that is, the length of a Martian day—is close to 24 terrestrial hours.[13]

ESSENTIAL CHARACTERISTICS OF THE PLANET MARS

In the three centuries since Huygens, the essential characteristics of Mars have been determined. The mean diameter of the red planet is roughly 4,170 miles, or slightly more than one-half the diameter of earth. The mass of Mars is only slightly more than one-tenth of earth's. In 1610 Kepler predicted—correctly, as it turned out—that Mars had two natural satellites or moons. These were not discovered by telescope, however, until 1877.[14] The two Martian moons are extremely small, and their orbits are extremely close to the parent planet. The inner satellite, Phobos, is 10 miles in diameter and orbits Mars at a distance of around 3,750 miles; the outer satellite, Deimos, is five miles in diameter and orbits at a distance of around 12,000 miles. Phobos requires only 7 hours and 39 minutes to complete a revolution of Mars; it is the only known satellite in the solar system with a period of revolution that is shorter than the rotational period of its parent planet. To an observer of Mars, Phobos would appear to rise and set twice a day.

Knowledge of the composition of Mars' atmosphere is incomplete even after the Mariner missions. Carbon dioxide is believed to be the major constituent. There are very small quantities of water vapor and possibly also some carbon monoxide. If the latter is present, then traces of oxygen and ozone are probably present also, but they have not been positively detected as yet.

The thinness of the Martian atmosphere makes for sharp day-night variations in surface temperature. Instrument readings taken by Mariner 6 found temperatures on the Martian equator to be "as comfortable as San Francisco" in

---

[13] Today, the length of the Martian day is accepted as about 24 hours, 37½ minutes.
[14] They were first sighted by an American, Asaph Hall, at the U. S. Naval Observatory in Washington, D. C.

the daytime and as cold as winter in Antarctica at night. That is, the range was between 70° F during the day and —100° F in nighttime.

Temperatures in Martian polar regions are considerably colder at night than at the equator, but it is not certain how much colder. The infrared spectrometer aboard Mariner 7 indicated that the polar temperature was cold enough to freeze water but too warm to freeze carbon dioxide. But a second Mariner 7 instrument, called an infrared radiometer, indicated that the temperature was close to the —253° F at which carbon dioxide would solidify in the Martian atmosphere. Gerry Neugebauer of the California Institute of Technology, the man in charge of the radiometer experiment, said on Aug. 7 that its data might be taken "as very strong circumstantial evidence that the polar caps are in fact predominately made of carbon dioxide, rather than water ice."

VARIABLE FEATURES OF THE MARTIAN LANDSCAPE

The polar caps of Mars, which advance in winter and retreat in summer, are only two of the planet's changeable features that have long intrigued earth-based astronomers. About two-thirds of the surface of Mars, as seen through a telescope, appears covered with brightly colored patches, some as large as continents on earth. The color of these regions ranges from brick red to deep rose to bright orange. Dark patches several hundred miles wide also are prominent on Mars. Their color, as viewed through a telescope, also is varied—grey, forest green or light green.

The bright and dark regions on Mars vary not only in color but also in shape and size. Over long periods of time, the dark regions will gradually expand or shrink, much as a desert on earth would do. But there are, in addition, apparently seasonal changes. In the summer certain dark areas begin to broaden and stretch into the surrounding bright regions. Then, as winter returns, these same regions withdraw to the approximate size and shape they were before. Seen from another planet, earth would display similar changes in its large forest areas and grassy plains.

Because of their color, the bright areas on Mars long were referred to as "deserts." Actually, they probably bear little if any resemblance to terrestrial deserts. It is now widely agreed that the color of the bright areas is attributable to the presence of hydrated ferric oxide (or oxides)—in other words, iron ore. There are differences of opinion, however, concerning the amount of such material on the Martian surface. It is believed possible that iron may have been deposited on the planet by meteorites from the asteroid belt, which is situated between Mars and Jupiter.

The dark areas on Mars were thought for many years to be bodies of water and hence were called maria, or seas. Although the color of the dark areas appears, as noted, to be greenish, it may actually be some other hue. C. F. Capen of the Jet Propulsion Laboratory and his associates used color filters in their observations of Mars in 1964-65. They reported that the dark areas reflected a host of colors—dark purple and brown, blue-green, green-blue, variegated gray and brown, dark gray, blue-gray, and gray-green. Studies of the wavelengths of light reflected from the light and the dark areas have led to speculation that the predominant color of both is red. If so, the apparent differences in color could be accounted for by differences in the size of surface particles. The dark areas, according to this hypothesis, are covered by relatively large particles which reflect less light than the smaller particles in the bright areas.

Explanations of changes in the size of Martian dark areas likewise are based largely on informed guesswork. An early and still appealing theory holds that the dark areas are indeed greenish, and that they consist of vegetation, perhaps of the primitive lichen type found on earth. The dark areas begin to expand at about the time the polar caps begin to recede. Thus, if the polar regions consist largely or even partly of water ice, it might be expected that gradual transfer of water vapor from higher to lower latitudes is responsible in some way for the increasing extent and apparently increasing verdancy of the dark regions.

But alternative explanations for the spread of the dark regions also have been offered. One of these holds that freezing of moisture in the soil during the Martian afternoon and evening increases the porosity and roughness of the soil and thus reduces its capacity to reflect light. A second explanation depends on the assumption of wind storms on Mars. V. V. Sharonov, a Soviet scientist, wrote in 1958: "The air currents in the [Martian] atmosphere vary from season to season, depositing dust at some times of the year and blowing it away at other times. Thus, for instance, the inherently dark surface . . . may brighten at a definite time of the year as a result of settling of light-colored dust blown over from the dessert areas." No single explanation of changes in Martian surface features, however, has been universally accepted.

SPECULATION ABOUT MARS BASED ON THE 'CANALS'

The so-called "canals" of Mars have aroused more curiosity and speculation among the public—if not among scientists—than any other feature of the planet. On the basis of telescopic observations in 1877, Giovanni V. Schiaparelli, an Italian astronomer, reported that the surface of Mars was criss-crossed by markings which he called *canali*. Some other astronomers jumped to the conclusion that the markings indicated the actual existence on Mars of canals constructed to transport water across the surface of the red planet in much the same way that irrigation ditches carry water to dry regions on earth.

To many astronomers Schiaparelli's canals meant one important thing. If there were such canals, surely there were intelligent beings who built them. And considering the size of the Martian canals, the intelligent beings must have belonged to an advanced civilization, for the canals represented a tremendous engineering feat. If one of these canals were moved to earth, it would stretch from New York to Texas and would be one hundred miles wide! Perhaps you can understand why some astronomers hesitated to take Schiaparelli's canals seriously. Yet others did take them seriously.[15]

A number of astronomers had rejected the existence of Martian canals because they could not see them on their telescopes. The American astronomer Percival Lowell built an observatory at Flagstaff, Ariz., and through its powerful telescope made an intensive study of the canals. In 1906 he elaborated on the theory that they were vast artificial waterways built by intelligent life. Lowell suggested that at some time the planet's water supply must have begun to fail. He thought the Martians must then have piped water into their cities from distant areas, but that later they were forced to construct a planet-wide irrigation system designed to tap water from the melting polar caps. Answering one obvious objection to this theory, Lowell suggested that the Martians must have constructed an extensive pumping system to force water through the canals; he even estimated that the power required would be 4,000 times that generated by Niagara Falls.

---

[15] Roy A. Gallant, *Exploring Mars* (1956), p. 22.

143

While Lowell's assumptions seem a little quaint and romantic today, he wrote in a flowery yet vigorous style that carried great persuasiveness. His impact on the public imagination hardly seems surprising in light of the fact that three decades later, in 1938, an Orson Welles radio broadcast of H. G. Wells' *The War of the Worlds*, a fictional account of an invasion from Mars, caused hundreds of persons in New York and New Jersey to flee their homes in terror.

Requirements of Planetary Exploration

A MANNED FLIGHT to Mars no doubt will be undertaken eventually, although perhaps not so soon as NASA officials might wish. In the meantime, however, several additional unmanned flights to the red planet, as well as several additional manned Apollo flights to the moon, already have been scheduled. Moreover, the late 1970s will afford a rare opportunity to mount an unmanned expedition to the planets beyond Mars—Jupiter, Saturn, Uranus, Neptune and Pluto.

UNMANNED FLIGHTS: FLYBYS, ORBITERS AND LANDERS

Mariners 4, 6 and 7 are referred to by space officials as "flybys" because they simply swept past Mars and continued on into outer space. But succeeding unmanned Mars probes will be more sophisticated and should provide more detailed information about the planet. Mariners 8 and 9, scheduled for launching in 1971, will be basically identical to the earlier flights in the series. Each, however, will carry a braking rocket that will fire in the vicinity of Mars, placing the craft in Martian orbit. Present plans call for the two Mariner orbiters to circle Mars for around three months, during which time they will photograph 70 per cent of the planet's surface and search for warm, moist areas where some form of life might be present. Such areas, if they are found to exist, presumably would be the target of two Viking spacecraft scheduled for launching in 1973. Each Viking is to consist of an orbiting capsule and a soft-landing laboratory capable of obtaining and analyzing Martian soil.

It is not yet known what method will be used for capturing the soil samples. A number of ideas have been suggested, including the use of sticky string to which surface particles will adhere, various types of suction devices, and the formation of very small particles in a gas (aerosol). Most of the proposed soil-gathering schemes would take material at or close to the surface. "It is not at all improbable, however, that if living organisms exist in the Martian soil, they will be found below the surface where they are protected from ultraviolet radiation and where the amount of water may exceed that nearer to the surface." [16]

Another problem in searching for life on Mars by means of instruments is that scientists are uncertain about what kind of organism to look for. Various chemical and optical tests for detecting Martian organisms have been proposed. All of the tests would evoke a positive response from terrestrial life. Whether or not life that had evolved on Mars would react in the same way is, however, far from assured. Because one or two tests might yield conflicting results, it is suggested that the Viking instrument laboratories contain as many different tests as possible.

NEED TO AVOID POLLUTION OF THE MARTIAN SURFACE

If the search for life on Mars is to have any significance, all conceivable steps will have to be taken to minimize or eliminate the possibility that the planet will become contaminated by terrestrial organisms. Micro-organisms are found in large numbers almost everywhere on earth. They would, as a result, be present on any Mars spacecraft or instruments unless special precautions were taken to destroy them prior to launching.

If such precautions were not taken, the possibility might arise that an instrument package landed on Mars for the purpose of detecting life would provide a source of contamination for its own experiments. In other words, the organisms detected might not necessarily be life forms indigenous to Mars but those carried to the planet from earth. An even more serious situation would arise if terrestrial organisms spread from the original point of contamination and multiplied on the surface of Mars. In that case, such organisms might be detected at a later date by a completely sterilized vehicle and mistaken for indigenous Martian life.

The importance of sterilizing spacecraft designed for planetary exploration was recognized in this country at the

---

[16] Samuel Glasstone, *op. cit.*, p. 227.

time the first satellites were placed in earth orbit. In February 1968, the council of the National Academy of Sciences expressed concern that early landings on the planets "might compromise and make impossible forever critical scientific experiments" and agreed to "plan lunar and planetary experiments . . . so as to prevent contamination of celestial objects in a way that would not impair the unique . . . scientific opportunities."

Eight months later, in October 1958, the Committee on Space Research, commonly known as COSPAR, was established by the International Council of Scientific Unions. In due course, COSPAR appointed a study group on standards for space probe sterilization,[17] which submitted recommendations that were adopted at a meeting of the parent organization in May 1964. One of the recommendations stipulated that no spacecraft should fly closer than 2,000 kilometers (1,250 miles) to the surface of Mars—a requirement met by the three Mariner probes launched to date. Specifications adopted for planetary landers state that the capsules should be sterilized to such an extent that there is not more than one chance in 10,000 of a single organism capable of reproduction remaining on them.

The instruments aboard a Mars lander must be able to operate, of course, after the drastic sterilization procedures that will be necessary prior to launching. In addition, the instruments must be light enough so that several can be carried in a single vehicle, and they must be capable of operating automatically or by remote control from earth. Finally, they must be rugged enough to remain undamaged after being dropped to the surface from a spacecraft, and they must not be adversely affected by the extreme daily variations in temperature.

PROSPECT OF ESTABLISHING HUMAN COLONY ON MARS

Looking beyond unmanned exploration of Mars, and even beyond manned exploration, some scientists have considered the possibility of colonizing the red planet. It is said that overpopulation, radioactive or other contamination, or a new ice age might make such a venture desirable or even imperative. The difficulties naturally would be immense, but they might not be insurmountable.

---

[17] Member countries were the United States, the Soviet Union, Great Britain, Sweden, Belgium, France.

Mission to Mars: Benefits Vs. Costs

The *Economist* of London pointed out on Aug. 2, 1969, that "technologists now believe that they are capable of manufacturing a human climate for Mars until the planet can sustain one for itself," although the process "might take a century." The *Economist* added that "If organic life is introduced onto Mars by man, and artificially fostered by him under protective domes until it can survive unaided outside, we may one day turn it from a red into a green planet."

Apart from excessive ultraviolet radiation and the cold nights, the temperature, light and gravity on Mars probably would be acceptable to human beings from earth. The thin atmosphere, low atmospheric pressure and scarcity of water would present more serious but not necessarily insuperable problems. At first, men from earth would have to live in closed structures on Mars. Assuming such structures could be built, it would be relatively easy to provide sufficient oxygen and heat. Water could be extracted from subsurface permafrost, if an adequate supply existed. If it did not, water might have to be transported from earth or extracted at great expense from minerals on or near the Martian surface.

Plants from earth presumably would thrive in the closed structures that would house men on Mars; indeed, they would help to provide the inhabitants with oxygen. Animals also could be raised. But animal husbandry would have to be carried out in the factory-like manner now employed on earth for chickens, eggs, and milk.

Opportunity for a 'Grand Tour' of Outer Planets

The chances of colonizing or finding life on planets other than Mars are considered extremely remote. Nevertheless, plans have been made to send unmanned spacecraft to several of the inner and outer planets in the 1970s. NASA intends to launch its first Mercury probe in 1973. Two years later, a multi-capsule spacecraft is scheduled to land at least one package of instruments on the torrid surface of Venus. In 1972 and 1973, a pair of spacecraft called Pioneer F and Pioneer G are to be sent toward Jupiter, the largest planet in the solar system. It is hoped that one or both of them will penetrate the planet's intense radiation belts and study its strange radio emissions.

147

Scientists are even more intrigued by the possibility of undertaking one or more "grand tours" of the outer planets —those beyond Mars—in the late 1970s. Between 1976 and 1980 the five outer planets will be so aligned as to permit a single spacecraft to explore several on the same flight. Such an alignment occurs roughly only once every 179 years.

James E. Long of the Jet Propulsion Laboratory's advanced studies office proposed in *Astronautics and Aeronautics Magazine*, June 1969, that two "grand tours" be launched. One would fly by Jupiter, Saturn and Pluto (the most distant planet) ; the other would go to Jupiter, Uranus and Neptune. Because of the vast distances involved, each flight would take up to nine years to complete. Spacecraft involved in such a long voyage would have to be capable of replacing failed equipment. Self-repairing computer and data-storage systems already are under development. In arguing that the grand tour project justifies high priority among future space projects, Long asserted that "The outer planets are extremely attractive subjects for extending present knowledge of the origin and evolution of the solar system as well as knowledge of interesting 'new worlds.' " The space science board of the National Academy of Sciences and the National Research Council, in a report issued Aug. 4, recommended that three grand tours [18] be undertaken between the late 1970s and early 1980s. The Space Task Group, as noted, also recommended flyby missions to the outer planets toward the end of the next decade.

It remains to be seen whether the excitement and urgency felt by scientists and space agency officials about interplanetary flight can be communicated to the American public and to Congress. Untold billions of dollars might well seem an exorbitant price to pay for acquisition of additional knowledge about the origin of the solar system. Even the discovery of rudimentary life on Mars might seem insufficient motivation for a manned flight to that planet. But man's unending curiosity and quest for knowledge may prove in the end to be a stronger emotion than the desire to economize on space exploration.

---

[18] Jupiter, Saturn, Pluto (1977); Jupiter, Uranus, Neptune (1979); Jupiter, Uranus (early 1980s).

Resolution of Conflicts

by

William Gerber

1 9 6 9
July 2

RESOLUTION OF CONFLICTS

T HE GREATEST HONOR history can bestow, President Nixon declared in his inaugural address, is "the title of peacemaker." Aspiring to earn that title, the President announced the method he intended to use in aiming to make peace. "After a period of confrontation," he said, "we are entering an era of negotiation."

The type of confrontation to which the President referred was that among nations, as in the Viet Nam war, and the negotiation he envisaged likewise would involve the representatives of nations, as in the current Paris peace talks. Negotiation, however, represents only one of an array of techniques, old and new, for resolving a wide variety of conflicts. These techniques, skillfully applied, can have a beneficial effect not only on international differences, but also on racial and ethnic tensions, divisiveness in cities and universities, polarization of economic classes, and the contemporary challenge to authority.

CONFLICT RESOLUTION: A NEW SOCIAL SCIENCE

The principles of conflict resolution are undergoing intensive analysis, study, and evaluation by behavioral experts in cooperation with administrators, mediators, counselors, psychiatrists, and diplomats. An article in *Newsweek*, Dec. 2, 1968, noted that "The task of conflict resolution has become a full-time occupation—and a major field of research." Need for the ministrations of this fledgling member of the social sciences has mounted in today's world, in part because of the declining effectiveness of force as a response to disruptiveness.

Refinement of the principles of conflict resolution is not merely a theoretical exercise for research seminars, although that in itself can contribute meaningfully to the understanding of struggle as a fact of life. Rather, this discipline shows signs of becoming one of the most practical of intellectual endeavors, offering opportunities for profitable application in a multitude of fields. Theodore W. Kheel, a prominent mediator of labor disputes, believes that its application is crucial in the present troubled times. As he wrote early this year: "Uncontained conflict now threatens to rip the fabric binding our society. The lesson of this past year is clear: We must improve our capacity to accommodate competing claims if we are to resolve community disputes. And we must find a way to resolve such disputes if we are to survive." [1]

Conflict as such is not necessarily undesirable. On the contrary, some forms of confrontation are salutary. As Ross Stagner, a research psychologist, has noted, "Individuals progress from infantilism to maturity as they encounter and solve conflicts." [2] Moreover, rivalry in athletic competitions, as well as in school, work, love, art, and politics, can extend the horizons of excellence. The Greek philosopher Heraclitus criticized Homer for wishing that strife might perish. According to Heraclitus, strife (or competition) is essential to progress. But conflict can also be destructive. It is that kind that threatens survival.

Musafer Sherif, a professor of social psychology at Pennsylvania State University, wrote in the *Washington Post*, June 1, 1969, that "Today, groups with contrasting notions of the world have, willy-nilly, become interdependent in numerous respects."

> In the area of weaponry, hence of future life itself, groups and nations are in a common predicament for human survival with human culture accumulated through centuries. Increasingly, the common predicament for human survival will become an overriding concern everywhere. . . . Probably it is unrealistic to hope that nations will soon cooperate on issues where their positions are already crystallized. . . . But each year the world changes and there are new issues on which the positions are not frozen.

As examples of such issues, Sherif cited the "twin problems of an exploding population and feeding the hungry."

RED TACTICS IN NEGOTIATING FOR VIET NAM PEACE

The current Paris peace talks offer a formidable challenge to President Nixon's abilities as a peacemaker. The Viet Nam war is the longest and one of the most bitter in American history, and the outlines of a settlement acceptable to all sides are not yet evident. Moreover, the record of Communist

---

[1] Theodore W. Kheel, "Collective Bargaining and Community Disputes," *Monthly Labor Review*, January 1969, p. 3.

[2] Introduction, in Ross Stagner (ed.), *The Dimensions of Human Conflict* (1967), p. 20.

behavior in past negotiations, particularly those that led to termination of the Korean War, suggests that the negotiators at Paris still have a long road to follow.

The Korean truce negotiations began at Kaesong, North Korea, on July 10, 1951, and continued for two years before agreement finally was reached on terms of the armistice signed at Panmunjom on July 27, 1953. Bitter and prolonged disagreements preceded every decision, however insignificant. Ten plenary sessions occupying a total of 17 days were required merely to reach agreement on the conference agenda.

Adm. C. Turner Joy, chief U.N. Command negotiator during most of the conference, has pointed out that the Communists sought an agenda "composed of *conclusions* favorable to their basic objectives" whereas the U.N. Command favored one which would be "only a list of topics to be discussed." Procrastination is a favorite Communist tactic when negotiating with Westerners. The Communists "hope to exploit to their advantage the characteristic impatience of Western peoples, impatience to complete a task once it has been begun," Joy has written. "This is a shrewd analysis, particularly as it applies to Americans." [3]

A similar pattern of behavior has emerged at the Paris peace talks. More than a month of haggling over a conference site preceded opening of preliminary peace talks in Paris on May 9, 1968. Since then, the United States has made concessions to the Communists—as it did at Kaesong —to break deadlocks in the negotiations. Four-party talks [4] were not agreed to until President Johnson brought the bombing of North Viet Nam to a halt last Nov. 1; the talks did not begin until Washington amended its position on seating arrangements; and now President Nixon has announced a limited withdrawal of American troops from Viet Nam. As was the case at Kaesong, the United States at Paris has appeared more eager than the Communists to reach a settlement, and the Communists have exploited this eagerness to the utmost.

BASIC GUIDELINES FOR MEDIATORS OR ARBITRATORS

For use in resolving conflicts which are destructive, many hypotheses have been formulated and put to the test. [5] Pre-

---

[3] Adm. C. Turner Joy, *How Communists Negotiate* (1955), pp. 18, 39.

[4] North Viet Nam, South Viet Nam, the United States, the National Liberation Front. The preliminary talks involved only the United States and North Viet Nam.

cepts found to produce generally favorable results may be summarized as follows:

(1) Try to prevent conflicts by watching for developing frustrations and doing everything possible to cope with them before they fester.

(2) When a conflict erupts, establish immediate communication with the disputants and keep the channels open, if possible, until the conflict is settled.

(3) Keep calm and seek agreement on a cooling-off period.[6]

(4) In international crises, conduct the most delicate negotiations in secret and insist that neither party disclose publicly its own or the opponent's tentative concessions until a measure of agreement has been reached.

(5) Study the temperament of the principal negotiator on the other side and adjust tactics accordingly.[7]

(6) Whenever possible, provide an alternative outlet for the disputant who is losing a major objective, especially if he is a leader negotiating for a group or a nation, because leaders find it difficult to obtain approval of compromises without some semblance of victory.

(7) If a conflict gives every evidence of being intractable, it is sometimes useful for the parties candidly to recognize that state of affairs.

(8) Identify interests common to the disputants and direct attention to those interests to the greatest possible extent.

(9) If a conflict is complex, try to fragment it. When smaller components are settled, it becomes easier to deal with the big ones.

(10) Where only two alternatives seem to exist, persist in trying to find others. Where each rival claims sole enjoyment of an indivisible possession or privilege, so that the only alternatives seem to be victory for A or victory for B, consider scheduling their exclusive right to the possession or privilege in sequence.

An example of the last-named solution was given by the U.N. General Assembly in 1963. When members could not agree on election of Czechoslovakia or Malaysia for a two-year term on the Security Council, they finally decided to let Czechoslovakia have the seat for the first year and Malaysia for the second year.

---

[5] Outstanding investigators in this field include Kenneth E. Boulding, an economics professor at the University of Colorado and one of the founders, when he was at the University of Michigan, of its Center for Research in Conflict Resolution; Anatol Rapoport, University of Michigan expert in decision theory; and Herman Kahn, director of the Hudson Institute, White Plains, N. Y.

[6] See "Labor Strife and the Public Interest," *E.R.R.*, 1966 Vol. II, pp. 775-778.

[7] Before President Kennedy conferred with Soviet Premier Khrushchev at Vienna in 1961, he was given pointers by a social psychiatrist who had made a study of Khrushchev's personality. He advised the President: "The direct handclasp, informality, and a willingness to tolerate physical proximity please him greatly—and lead to such 'trust in the man' as he is capable of. . . . Khrushchev tolerates disagreement perfectly well, especially when it is stated as such; thus, 'I disagree with you on that' or 'we see things differently.' . . . But attempts to explain, persuade, or convince are useless."—Bryant Wedge, M.D. (director, Institute for the Study of National Behavior, West Medford, Mass.), "Khrushchev at a Distance—A Study of Public Personality," *Trans-action*, October 1968, pp. 26-27.

Resolution of Conflicts

Alternatives to victory by either contestant can sometimes best be developed by someone having nothing to gain from the outcome of the conflict. Such a person can make new proposals without losing face, serve as a target for disputants who need to blow off steam, and approach the problem free of emotional blindness. The very act of introducing a neutral party in a situation filled with hostility tends to ease tension.

GOOD OFFICES AND OTHER THIRD-PARTY ASSISTANCE

The device of third-party assistance, known as good offices, is at the bottom of the ladder of conflict resolution. It involves simply a tender of service by an outsider in adjusting the difference in any way that the parties may find acceptable. It is valuable in that it often leads to other kinds of third-party help, including conciliation, which is a rung above good offices. A conciliator listens to both sides, tries to clear up misunderstandings, and performs fact-finding services if the parties so desire.

On the middle rungs of the ladder are various forms of mediation. "The mediator," two social scientists have pointed out, "tries to stimulate counterproposals, compromises, and concessions by bringing up new ideas, by suggesting new combinations of compromises and concessions, and by serving as a vehicle for communication regarding extremely delicate points."[8] William E. Simkin, director of the Federal Mediation and Conciliation Service from 1961 to January 1969, has listed some of the ways in which a mediator operates:

> A mediator . . . can bring the parties together when they otherwise would not meet. He can separate them when he senses that an explosion is imminent. He can blunt personality clashes. He can "try on for size" possible solutions that one of the parties would not suggest "across the table" for strategic reasons. . . . He can help clear away diversions and prod the disputants to face up to their joint responsibility.[9]

The chances for success are greater if the mediator is involved at an early stage, before "the relationship between the negotiating parties has degenerated to a sustained and hostile debate, and the respective teams have assumed final hard-line positions."[10]

---

[8] William E. Stiles and Edward L. Robran, "Dealing With Impasse," *Today's Education*, January 1969, p. 57.

[9] William E. Simkin, "Union-Management Conflicts—Some Aspects of Resolution," in Ross Stagner (ed.), *op. cit.*, p. 103.

[10] William E. Stiles and Edward L. Robran, *op. cit.*, p. 57.

In cases of arbitration, the neutral party is given full authority. The question in dispute is submitted to him with the understanding that his decision will be accepted as binding. Although the third party thus has the deciding voice in settling the dispute, the contending parties must first reach agreement not only on the exact question or questions to be submitted for arbitration, but also on the choice of an arbitrator, and on the rules under which the proceedings will be conducted. International law recognizes the right of one or both parties, in a dispute between nations, to reject an award on grounds of "manifest injustice." Despite that limitation, arbitration has been successful in resolving a large number of disputes between nations, and it has proved of value in resolving labor-management controversies and in settling damage claims.

The American Arbitration Association, with headquarters in New York, has been serving since 1926 as a source of arbitrators for persons, companies, or organizations involved in civil disputes. Its National Panel of Arbitrators contains 16,000 names. The number of cases in which disputants requested and received the services of the association rose from about 3,500 in 1957 to about 17,000 in 1968.

With financial assistance from the Ford Foundation, the association in 1968 established in Washington, D.C., a Center for Dispute Settlement. The center recruits and trains arbitrators and puts disputants in touch with them. It already has helped to resolve conflicts between students and university administrators, landlords and tenants, welfare agencies and clients, merchants and consumers, employers and employees, and government agencies and civil rights groups.

LIMITATIONS OF VIOLENCE AS THE ULTIMATE ARBITER

A major purpose of developing effective techniques of conflict resolution is to prevent resort to violence. Settlement of disputes by violence is inherently wrong, and it tends to weaken one of the foundations of civilization, namely, settlement by legal process of otherwise irreconcilable disputes.

Resolution of conflicts by persuasion has been cherished as an ideal since ancient times. Mahavira, founder of the Jain religion in India in the sixth century B.C., forbade lethal violence, whether in conflict, for holy sacrifice, or otherwise. In Judaism, the commandment not to kill was elevated by the Essene sect in the first century B.C. to an injunction against all violence and, when smitten on one cheek, to offer the other. The Roman Catholic Church, after several centuries of ambivalence in countenancing the ultimate violence of war, tried to avoid the dilemma by distinguishing between just and unjust wars.

The Reformation produced a number of sects, including the Mennonites and the Quakers (or Friends), that completely rejected participation in war. In the 19th century, William Lloyd Garrison, Henry David Thoreau, and Leo Tolstoy advocated nonviolent resistance as a means of combating international and social injustice without engaging in conflict. The more recent period produced two illustrious preachers of nonviolence, Mohandas K. Gandhi and Martin Luther King Jr. Gandhi told a visiting American Negro leader, Dr. Howard Thurman, in 1936 that "It may be through the Negroes that the unadulterated message of nonviolence will be delivered to the world." [11] King acknowledged Gandhi as the source of his own philosophy of nonviolence.

Enthusiasm in the civil rights movement for passive (nonviolent) resistance as an instrument of persuasion reached a peak in the United States during the 1950s. The decade of the 1960s has been marked on the one hand by widespread resort to violence by militant Negro and student minorities [12] and, on the other hand, by significant resistance to service in the war in Viet Nam.[13] The case against violence as a means of bringing about changes in the structure of society was summarized by the Rev. John M. Swomley, professor of social ethics at the St. Paul School of Theology in Kansas City. "The most successful revolution in modern history," Swomley wrote, "is the Gandhian, which not only set India free but started a chain reaction that ended colonialism in almost every place it existed"; while in every violent revolution since 1917 "the more violence, the greater the degree of counter-revolution and hence the greater need for totalitarian controls." [14]

---

[11] Homer A. Jack, *The Gandhi Reader* (1956), p. 316. See "Mass Demonstrations," *E.R.R.*, 1963 Vol. II, pp. 601-602.

[12] See "Violence in American Life," *E.R.R.*, 1968 Vol. II, pp. 405-424.

[13] See "Resistance to Military Service," *E.R.R.*, 1968 Vol. I, pp. 201-220.

[14] John M. Swomley, "Violence and the Black Ghettoes," *Current Issues*, March 1969, pp. 1-2.

Milestones in the Reduction of Strife

THE LIFE OF MAN before the beginnings of civil society, Thomas Hobbes (1588-1679) said, was tantamount to a war of all against all, because exercise of physical power was then virtually the only available method of settling conflicts. Civil society provided a means of adjudicating differences in return for imposition of limits on individual freedom. John Locke (1632-1704) held that the main purpose of civil society was to preserve life, liberty, and property through concentration of power in an impartial rule-making and rule-enforcing authority. Locke's philosophy was absorbed by the fathers of the American constitutional and legal system.

The oldest known set of principles for public adjudication of conflicts is the law code promulgated in Babylonia around 1800 B.C. by King Hammurabi. It prescribed ways of settling disputes over property, the family, labor, and personal injuries. Other codifications of social norms of ancient Asia and the Middle East include the Biblical Book of Deuteronomy (seventh century B.C.), which contained the Ten Commandments and other moral and religious injunctions; the Analects of Confucius (551-479 B.C.), which stressed politeness toward adversaries; and the Laws of Manu (perhaps about 150 B.C.), which dealt in part with disputes between persons of the same and of different Indian castes. In the Western world, important summations of law were the Twelve Tables (about 450 B.C.), which limited the power of Roman patricians in resolving their differences with plebeians; Justinian's Code (sixth century A.D.), a compilation of statutes, legal opinions, and principles of judicial settlement; Magna Carta (1215), which regulated differences between the King and feudal barons; and the Code Napoléon (1804), which aimed at providing adjudication on egalitarian principles.

Over the centuries, there developed the idea of judicial settlement of conflicts not only through interpretation of applicable written statutes and previous court decisions, but also—especially where no statute or judicial decision was applicable—on the basis of equity. In England, litigants disappointed over the outcome of common law cases turned to the King and the Lord Chancellor in so many instances that there evolved, in the 14th century, a special institution, the court of chancery, for settlement of civil suits in the interests of equity. The Congress of the United States gave to the federal courts established under the Constitution jurisdiction in both law and equity, and the several states either gave similar authority to state courts or established separate courts of equity.[15]

In every civilized land and era, judicial settlement, whether formal or founded on equity, has been one of the most successful amenities of human society. However, the modern system of legal justice, penology, and police power contains many areas in which it is recognized that improvement is needed. Such improvement was one of the objectives of two commissions appointed by President Lyndon B. Johnson to study, among other things, the role of police officers in controlling conflicts. First of the two groups was the National Advisory Commission on Civil Disorders, appointed July 27, 1967, with Gov. Otto Kerner of Illinois as chairman. The Kerner commission said in its report on Feb. 29, 1968:

> The abrasive relationship between the police and the minority communities has been a major—and explosive—source of grievance, tension and disorder. . . . The police are faced with demands for increased protection and service in the ghetto. Yet the aggressive patrol practices thought necessary to meet these demands themselves create tension and hostility. . . . The Commission recommends that city government and police authorities review police operations in the ghetto to ensure proper conduct by police officers, and eliminate abrasive practices.

The second group was the Commission on the Causes and Prevention of Violence in the United States, appointed June 5, 1968 (after the assassination of Sen. Robert F. Kennedy), with Milton S. Eisenhower as chairman. The commission on Dec. 1, 1968, released without evaluation or comment a report prepared by one of its panels on the demonstrations in Chicago during the 1968 Democratic National Convention. The panel, headed by Daniel Walker, president of the Chicago Crime Commission, charged that actions of some policemen in coping with the demonstrators amounted to a "police riot."

DEMOCRACY AND THE PRINCIPLE OF MAJORITY RULE

Settlement of conflicts through legal processes is supplemented, in countries with representative government, by

---

[15] British chancery and common law courts were amalgamated in 1873. In the United States, almost all of the state equity courts likewise have been merged with the regular courts.

application of the principle of majority rule, with irreducible rights for minorities. Majority rule has been a prime element of conflict resolution in enlightened societies since the foundation of democracy in ancient Athens. Applied to selection of legislators, administrative leaders, and some judges, the principle gives the majority its way, but assures the minority that it will have the right to try to replace incumbent officials at the next election.

Likewise in the legislative process, democracy offers the opportunity to adjust divergent viewpoints through majority rule with minority rights of persuasion. Here there is the added requirement that no legislation may curtail the basic rights of minorities and individuals as set forth in a constitution or other organic law. No democracy in history has been perfect, but impressive progress has been made toward accommodation of a range of conflicting social philosophies through legislative debate and decision.

EFFORTS TO KEEP OR MAKE PEACE AMONG NATIONS

In international affairs, a supreme governmental authority with power to enforce its decisions is lacking. This being so, and the destructive potentialities of international violence being what they are, Arthur J. Goldberg recently was moved to say: "Perhaps no subject is as critical as the question of how the U. S. and the international community will face and control conflicts which will inevitably arise in the 1970s." [16]

Of the many methods of facing and controlling international differences, negotiation by emissaries with full powers is one of the oldest and continues to have prime importance.[17] Other forms of negotiation include summit diplomacy and debate and discussion in international organizations. Negotiation accompanied by a show of force is sometimes called gunboat diplomacy, but this is virtually a negation of the concept. According to Prof. Kenneth E. Boulding, "One does not negotiate from strength; one may dictate from strength, but one does not negotiate." [18]

Settlement of international disputes with third-party assistance, which also has had a long history, occurs in the form of good offices, conciliation, and mediation; judicial

---

[16] Arthur J. Goldberg (chairman of the board, United Nations Association of the United States), preface in Kingman Brewster Jr. and others, *Controlling Conflicts in the 1970s* (1969), p. 2.

[17] See "State Department and Policy Making," *E.R.R.*, 1968 Vol. I, pp. 465-484.

[18] Kenneth E. Boulding, *Conflict and Defense; A General Theory* (1962), p. 323.

settlement; and arbitration. An outstanding instance of mediation was President Theodore Roosevelt's action in bringing Japan and Russia together to negotiate the treaty, signed in 1905 at Portsmouth, N. H., ending the Russo-Japanese War. Judicial settlement of international differences now is carried out mainly by the International Court of Justice at The Hague. However, the Court's powers are limited by the fact that the United States and some other countries have not accepted the optional clause of the Court's statute, which recognizes the Court's jurisdiction in "all legal disputes."

One of the most famous cases of international arbitration was the settlement by a five-country arbitral commission, a century ago, of American claims against Great Britain for depredations on Union shipping during the Civil War by the *Alabama* and other vessels built in England for the Confederacy. The arbitral commission awarded $15.5 million to the United States in damages.

The dream of an international organization powerful enough to resolve all conflicts between nations without war has appealed to many men of vision. The League of Nations lacked the required strength, and efforts to equip the United Nations for that task, while more successful, have fallen far short of the goal.[19] A recent suggestion for strengthening U.N. war-prevention capacities called for "establishment of a standby United Nations peacekeeping force of 20,000 to 50,000 men, composed of land, sea and air units from nonpermanent members" of the Security Council, while the permanent members would "provide logistic support for specified types of situations."[20]

Experts in conflict resolution have investigated strategic and social aspects of the problem of handling international conflicts. Herman Kahn has said that turning the other cheek may sometimes be not only morally but also tactically desirable in international conflicts:

> There has been much interest recently in the general use of de-escalatory tactics or moves. . . . A carefully hedged and limited "turning the other cheek" is argued not (or not only) out of moral . . . motivations but for instrumental reasons: it is put forward as

---

[19] See "United Nations Peacekeeping," *E.R.R.*, 1964 Vol. II, pp. 609-620.

[20] Kingman Brewster Jr. and others, *op. cit.*, pp. 41, 43. The panel that made the suggestion consisted of Brewster, who is president of Yale University, Gen. Matthew B. Ridgway, Cyrus R. Vance, Jerome J. Wiesner, Charles W. Yost, and 21 other prominent Americans.

a prudent or advantageous method of dealing with an opponent. . . .
It is argued that unilateral initiatives might be used to call forth
similar initiatives from the opponent.[21]

Another factor, in addition to unilateral self-restraint, which
was found to militate against escalation in a study of 45
conflicts is "a strong world opinion . . . demanding a cease-
fire, negotiation, or renunciation of its cause by one party."[22]
Prof. Boulding, appraising efforts to establish the rule of
law in international relations, has held out hope of progress:
"The great course of political evolution, from the family to
the tribe to the nation to the superpower, and finally, one
hopes, to the world government now in its birth pangs, is
testimony to the ability of human organization to extend
conflict control to wider and wider areas."[23]

OMBUDSMAN AS NEGOTIATOR FOR AGGRIEVED CITIZENS

The government of a country faces in two directions.
Looking outward, it may come into conflict with another sov-
ereign state; looking inward, it confronts individual citizens.
The Roman republic, aiming to assist individuals who felt
that the government was being heavy-handed toward them,
established the office of tribune of the people. The law required the tribune to leave his door open at all times, so that
the injured and oppressed might find refuge with him at any
hour of need.

In modern times, the Swedish government was the first to
assign to a designated officer, called the ombudsman (commissioner), the duty of helping private citizens adversely
affected by administrative decisions. That action, taken in
1713, was followed initially by similar moves on the part of
Denmark, Finland, and Norway and in later years by other
countries, including the United Kingdom, where complaints
must be channeled through a member of Parliament; the
Soviet Union and other East European countries, where a
procurator receives complaints from individuals about viola-
tions of law by administrative agencies; and seven countries
in other parts of the world.[24]

Comparable to the right of submitting grievances to an
ombudsman is the privilege accorded by U. S. Army regulations to all soldiers to register complaints directly with the

---

[21] Herman Kahn, *On Escalation; Metaphors and Scenarios* (1965), p. 238.

[22] Quincy Wright, "The Escalation of International Conflicts," *Journal of Conflict
Resolution*, December 1965, p. 442.

[23] Kenneth E. Boulding, *op. cit.*, p. 324.

[24] Guyana, Israel, Japan, Malaysia, New Zealand, the Philippines, and Singapore.

Office of the Inspector General instead of taking them up with immediate superiors. In addition, about 30 universities in the United States have ombudsmen to protect students from bureaucratic excesses. A Senate Judiciary subcommittee held hearings in 1966 and 1968 on bills to establish a federal office of ombudsman, but no further action was taken.

Those in favor of the ombudsman concept contend that such an officer "can help overcome the increasing depersonalization and alienation between citizens and their governments." [25] It is also argued that although the ombudsman cannot remedy basic injustices, we should "at least try in a civilized way to take care of the grievances, while remembering to attack the other problems as well." [26] It has been suggested that the system be appraised during a trial period: "Its introduction at the state level would permit experimentation with the institution before possible adoption at the higher level of government." [27]

Conflict Areas in Need of Recurring Aid

SYSTEMATIC EFFORTS at conflict resolution are regularly and extensively applied in the field of labor-management relations. Such efforts are essential in a field in which there is an enduring conflict of interests between two sides. The efforts do not end the basic conflict, but they settle any number of particular disputes. And because the possibility of controversy is ever present, there is constant search for more effective methods of dealing with it.

A distinguished labor mediator has pointed out that "Even though it comes under attack from time to time, especially when a strike threatens to inconvenience the public, this system of collective bargaining works far better than most people realize, producing agreements and stable relationships in more than 99 per cent of all negotiations." [28] Labor-man-

[25] Paul J. Weber, S.J., "A Friend at City Hall," *America*, Oct. 19, 1968, p. 354.

[26] Walter Gellhorn (professor of law, Columbia University), "The Ombudsman's Relevance to American Municipal Affairs," *American Bar Association Journal*, February 1968, p. 140.

[27] Ingunn N. Means, "The Norwegian Ombudsman," *Western Political Quarterly*, December 1968, p. 650.

[28] Theodore W. Kheel, *op. cit.*, p. 3.

agement differences are recurrent and grievous, but in the main they are resolved through negotiation. The prospect for further progress in avoidance of labor strife appears reasonably good, but strikes involving serious losses to both sides, intense mutual hostility, and shortages of services and goods will undoubtedly occur when methods of conflict resolution are not skillfully applied.

MACHINERY TO DEAL WITH LABOR CONTROVERSIES

Laws enacted by the federal government and 45 states make mediation services available for management and labor. In a few cases, preliminary use of these services is required before trade union leaders may call on their members to strike. The first American enactment providing public mediation services for labor disputes was a Maryland law of 1878. When Congress established the Department of Labor in 1913, it authorized appointment of conciliation commissioners to assist in settlement of employer-employee controversies. A mandatory cooling-off period associated with mediation was enacted for a single industry by the Railway Act of 1926, which, as amended in 1934 and 1936, provided that whenever a railroad (or air carrier since 1936) dispute has not yielded to mediation and a strike is threatened, the President may appoint an emergency board. The board has 30 days in which to investigate the dispute and make recommendations for its settlement. No strike may be called during the period of mediation or investigation or for 30 days after an emergency board has reported.

The most important federal legislation designed to assist in settling labor conflicts is the Labor-Management Relations (Taft-Hartley) Act of 1947. That law established a Federal Mediation and Conciliation Service and made the service independent of the Department of Labor. It provided also for a mandatory cooling-off period of 80 days to avert strikes which would "imperil the national health or safety."

The Mediation and Conciliation Service took cognizance, during the fiscal year ended June 30, 1968, of over 18,000 cases in which collective bargaining was seemingly about to break down. Assistance provided by the service led to resolution of the differences without a strike in all except 2,351 cases (12.5 per cent of the total).

More than 93 per cent of all U. S. collective bargaining agreements contain clauses providing for voluntary arbitration of labor disputes. About 30,000 labor arbitrations took place in 1968, the arbitrators being nominated in many instances by the Federal Mediation and Conciliation Service or by the American Arbitration Association. Although arbitration has successfully resolved many labor conflicts, the *Wall Street Journal* observed editorially on Jan. 7, 1969: "Arbitration . . . is unlikely to produce equity in any objective sense. Arbitrators often seem to feel that their task is to produce peace, almost at any price. So their inclination all too frequently is to split the difference between the parties, no matter how reasonable or unreasonable either side may be."

Compulsory arbitration of labor disputes, established by law in Australia, New Zealand, and some other jurisdictions, has not completely ended strikes in those places but has generally resulted in avoidance of long and costly work stoppages. Accordingly, the question of making arbitration of labor-management conflicts compulsory in the United States has often been raised. But organized labor, always a vigilant guardian of the right to strike, strongly opposes any except the narrowest infringement of that right. Its opposition to compulsory arbitration is shared currently by Secretary of Labor George P. Shultz and business leaders on the ground that it would undermine collective bargaining and encourage the weaker of the negotiating parties to look to the government for resolution of many labor conflicts.

HARD PROBLEMS IN PROMOTION OF RACIAL HARMONY

Arbitration by a neutral third party is scarcely available for settlement of conflicts in race relations. Everyone is either Caucasion or non-Caucasian, and so there are no neutrals. The root cause of current racial unrest and militancy was identified bluntly by the National Advisory Commission on Civil Disorders (Kerner Commission) as white racism. "White racism," the commission asserted, "is essentially responsible for the explosive mixture which has been accumulating in our cities since the end of World War II."

Efforts to eliminate racial discrimination have taken several forms, including the 1955 bus boycott in Montgomery, Ala., where segregated seating was the issue; nonviolent sit-ins and marches led or inspired by the late Martin Luther King Jr.; and voting registration drives among Negroes in the South. Persuasion and psychological pressure were consciously chosen in that period as the principal weapons in the battle to improve the status of black Americans.

165

However, a sprinkling of influential black leaders began to argue that nonviolent pressure was not enough. Rioting, including arson, began to spread from city to city in black ghetto areas. The Kerner Commission, warning that the United States was "moving toward two societies, one black, one white—separate but unequal," called for a "massive and sustained" commitment to ameliorative measures transcending the new civil rights laws. But that recommendation did not receive White House or congressional support. Meanwhile, some black leaders put forward demands based on the ideal of black separatism.

Two Princeton professors stressed the right of Negroes to reject white, middle-class values. They designated as "cultural assimilationism" the view "that, in order to be accepted into mainstream America, minority groups have to divest themselves of their cultural values and manifest the value of the model American, namely, the white Anglo-Saxon Protestant." [29] In the ferment resulting from hatred of white values, some black militants exhibited a "Samson complex," saying in effect: "If we aren't treated right, we'll bring the whole structure down. Blacks will suffer, but many more whites will be hurt!" [30] The National Association for the Advancement of Colored People deplored the Samson complex and stressed constructive laws and community action to combat racial antipathies.

TRIAL AND ERROR IN HANDLING TURMOIL IN COLLEGES

Racial differences and differences between students and college administrators merged on a number of college campuses. Moreover, the alignment of opponents was complicated by the mixed allegiance of faculty members, numbers of whom sympathized with student demands for immediate, drastic change. It might have been thought that disputes between students and educational administrators would provide fertile ground for application of principles of conflict resolution, because both sides were presumably alert to the findings of psychologists and social scientists pertaining to social conflict. But it is taking a long time for the two sides to become aware of their respective responsibilities in the effort to find an accommodation of views.

---

[29] Vernon J. Dixon and M. Reginald Lewis, "Black Consciousness, Societal Values, and Educational Institutions: A Statement of Linkages," *Journal of Conflict Resolution*, September 1968, p. 402.

[30] St. Claire Drake (professor of sociology, Roosevelt University), "Urban Violence and American Social Movements," in Robert H. Connery (ed.), *Urban Riots; Violence and Social Change* (1968), p. 24.

Cool heads on both sides believe that it is the responsibility of college administrators to listen, take suggestions seriously, and avoid tokenism in adoption of viable reforms, while students have the responsibility to be civil, to allow others to be heard, and to respect the power of reason more than that of physical force. Buell G. Gallagher, president of the City College of New York until his resignation on May 9, made the following statement for a newspaper roundup of administrators' views on campus unrest in the New York area: "Many of the desires of students have merit, and many institutions change too slowly. Nevertheless, the right answer lies not in threat and counterthreat, violence and counterforce. It lies in mutual search for commonly accepted answers." [31]

President Nixon on Feb. 24, 1969, commended the president of Notre Dame University for on-the-spot expulsion of students who persisted in disruption after a warning. But an editorial in a Catholic weekly declared:

> The policy of threat decreed from Notre Dame University by its president, Father Theodore Hesburgh, is delusionary. . . . Students are to be taught in what amounts to an atmosphere of benevolent repression, with the administration shielded from all save the mildest of pressures from students frequently more sensitive to social and political urgencies than the university's august directors. It is an arrangement which impoverishes the university. The student witness is minimized and nothing more enlightened is expected from the administration than the policies which are the sickness of the nation and the very causes of really serious campus confrontations: institutional racism, exploitation of science, collusion with the military. [32]

Greater emphasis by university authorities on communicating with student rebels and less readiness to call in the police were important factors in peaceful termination of sit-ins at Brandeis University in January 1969 and at Columbia University at the end of April. Both faculty and students at Columbia felt that in the April 1969 sit-in Acting President Andrew W. Cordier, a former United Nations official experienced in crisis management, played his hand with consummate skill. He induced the radicals to leave occupied buildings by keeping cool and serving them with court orders instead of calling in the police.

---

[31] *New York Times*, May 1, 1969, p. 42.
[32] "Hesburgh's Law," *Commonweal*, March 14, 1969, pp. 719-720.

Jobs for the future

by

William Gerber

1 9 6 9
Dec. 10

JOBS FOR THE FUTURE

YOUNG PEOPLE entering the world of work in the next decade will have had, on the average if present trends continue, a sharply increased number of years of education. And they will expect to obtain jobs which provide not only security and status but also stimulation, outlets for creativity, and opportunities for frequent advancement. The aspirations of the restless new generation will confront society with the task of trying to ensure sufficient job openings despite the economy's ability to get more work done with fewer workers; and there will be need to try also to provide the new labor-force entrants with an exciting atmosphere in which to work.

Along with extended education for the many, the 1970s will see continuance, if not intensification, of the school dropout problem in the inner city. Dropouts will have a particularly hard time because youths under 18 or 20 years of age are virtually excluded from meaningful employment in a country which expects young people to remain in school.[1] It will therefore be important to find new ways to encourage dropouts to take special training in line with their capacities and with the requirements of employers.

In the context of rapid technological and social changes in the world of work, the question often is asked, For what should we be educating our young people? This question applies as much to those who remain in school as to those who drop out and need special training. Competent observers, without belittling the value of the humanities, contend that many aspects of today's curriculum are not in keeping with the times. They think the educational system lags seriously behind changes in social values and structures. According to one investigator, teachers do not know how to relate their subject "to the rest of knowledge, as well as to life." He points out that "In large part, this is what our student rebels

---

[1] See "Jobs for Young People," *E.R.R.*, 1961 Vol. II, pp. 505-509.

are complaining about: . . . relevance."[2] It is widely believed, moreover, that the system of occupational guidance in schools and colleges is inadequate and out of date.

To give the country's young people better preparation for earning a livelihood, to make counseling in the choice of a vocation available to many more of them than at present, and to assure job openings commensurate with their abilities and interests are pivotal tasks for the years ahead. The political fortunes of the Nixon administration may depend not only on disentanglement from the conflict in Viet Nam, but also on the availability of job opportunities and on the effectiveness of programs for manpower training and job placement. A manpower expert has pointed out that the number of men and women entering the labor force in the decade ending in 1975 will show "the largest . . . upturn for a ten-year period in our history."[3]

EDUCATIONAL BACKGROUND OF NEW JOB-SEEKERS

As far as classroom training is concerned, the level of achievement of Americans coming of age is rising steadily. Recipients of bachelor's or advanced degrees at American colleges and universities in the 10 years from 1969 to 1978 are expected to number around 8.5 million, compared with 4.9 million in the preceding 10-year period. Virtually all of these graduates, other than those who enter the Armed Forces, continue studying, or become housewives, will join the labor force.

The relationship of an advanced degree to success in business was indicated by a survey which the magazine *Careers Today* conducted, over a year ago, among 230 company presidents and 1,500 executives of 500 large concerns. Some 21 per cent of the men at the top, at that time, had earned doctorates, and it was expected that the figure would reach 30 per cent within a year. Of those who had achieved the most rapid advancement, 75 per cent had combined a master's degree in business administration with an undergraduate degree in science or engineering.

About 400,000 of today's undergraduates are black. They constitute 6 per cent of the college population, whereas

---

[2] Charles E. Silberman, quoted in the *New York Times*, Jan. 26, 1969, p. 48. See also "Reorganization of the Universities," *E.R.R.*, 1968 Vol. II, pp. 605-606.

[3] Seymour L. Wolfbein (Temple University), *The Emerging Labor Force; A Strategy for the Seventies* (1969), p. 4.

Jobs for the Future

PROJECTION OF DEGREES AWARDED
IN SELECTED YEARS

	Bachelor's and first professional degrees	Master's degrees	Doctorates (excluding M.D.s)
1968	685,000	148,800	22,200
1969	749,000	160,000	25,100
1970	746,000	190,400	26,500
1972	785,000	212,000	29,200
1974	860,000	226,900	38,900
1976	931,000	253,200	40,600
1978	980,000	273,700	43,900

SOURCE: U. S. Office of Education, *Projections of Educational Statistics to 1977-78* (1969), p. 31. Based on assumption that ratio of degrees to population will continue the 1958-66 trend.

Negroes make up 11.5 per cent of the total population. The number of nonwhite college students has increased dramatically in the past two years, but the level of educational attainment in the black population as a whole is distinctly lower than that of whites. Among persons 25 years old or older in 1967, 20.2 per cent of the Negroes as against 32.8 per cent of the whites were high school graduates; and 4 per cent of the Negroes as against 10.6 per cent of the whites were college graduates. Industry recently has launched vigorous efforts to recruit black college graduates.

The current generation of college graduates is spirited, socially conscious, and given to unconventional thinking. William S. Rukeyser, an associate editor of *Fortune*, has written of those who enter the business world:

> Educated people are bringing impressive skills to business, and making equally impressive demands. Companies wise enough to accommodate to both are reaping profits. But along the way they have had to up-end everything from training programs and organization charts to salary scales and the way top executives allocate their time. . . . Young employees are demanding that they be given productive tasks to do from the first day of work and that the people they work for notice and react to their performance.

Rukeyser added: "This is disturbing bureaucratic peace in some companies, but the results could be beneficial all around."[4]

PREPONDERANCE OF OPENINGS IN SERVICE SECTOR

The kinds of work available to tomorrow's high school or college graduates and other job-seekers will differ significantly from work being done today. The differences result

---

[4] William S. Rukeyser, "How Youth Is Reforming the Business World," *Fortune*, January 1969, pp. 77-79.

173

from advancing technology, increased education, and changing values. Technology creates new occupations, raises the demand for people in some lines of work, and reduces the demand in others. Expanded education multiplies job openings for teachers, educational administrators, and producers of educational materials. Changes in values have stimulated demand for travel agents, bus drivers, entertainers, waiters, barmaids, artists, engineers, doctors, and baby-sitters.

The latest Dictionary of Occupational Titles (published by the U. S. Department of Labor in two volumes in 1965) lists 21,741 separate occupations from able seaman to zylomounter (mounter of lenses in zylo-plastic eyeglass frames). The occupations in which demand is growing fastest are those involving work with people and ideas; that is, nonproduction jobs, rather than the goods-producing work of agriculture, mining, manufacturing, and construction.[5]

On an unidentified day in 1956, a celebrated breakthrough occurred in the United States, when two lines of occupational growth—production jobs and nonproduction jobs—crossed. On that day, for the first time in any modern country, more people were employed in nonproduction (white-collar or service) jobs than in production (blue-collar or farm) jobs. "Service employment," as noted by the Chase Manhattan Bank, "accounts for 88 per cent of total employment growth in the postwar period."[6]

The shift to service work results in part from applications of technology which enable farms and factories to produce a larger output with the same number of workers or with fewer workers. This development raises a question that is still unsettled: whether automation and other advances in technology lead to unemployment for the less educated, by abolishing more manual jobs (usually production jobs) than they create and by shifting the emphasis to white-collar work.[7] Some economists contend that availability of jobs, whether for the less educated or the better educated, depends primarily not on technology but on such factors as strong

---

[5] "Nonproduction jobs" include (1) all jobs in the non-goods-producing sectors of the economy; namely, transportation, communication, trade, finance, government, education, medicine, law, advertising, and others; and (2) nonproduction jobs (those of executives, clerks, salesmen, etc.) in the goods-producing sectors; namely, agriculture, mining, manufacturing, and construction.

[6] "Services in the U. S. Economy," *Business in Brief* (bank newsletter), February 1969, p. 5.

[7] See "Cushioning of Automation," *E.R.R.*, 1963 Vol. II, pp. 781-782.

Jobs for the Future

PROSPECTIVE CHANGES IN EMPLOYMENT

(per cent distribution)

	1960	1980
Goods-producing jobs	(40.8)	(33.2)
Manufacturing	25.6	22.6
Agriculture	8.7	3.6
Construction	5.6	6.5
Mining	0.9	0.5
Service-producing jobs	(59.2)	(66.8)
Trade	19.6	19.0
Services	17.0	22.0
Government	11.8	16.0
Transportation, communications, public utilities	6.4	4.4
Finance, insurance, real estate	4.4	5.4

SOURCE: Edgar L. Morphet and Charles O. Ryan (eds.), *Prospective Changes in Society by 1980* (1966), p. 99.

consumer purchasing power, expanding industrial demand, and economic growth.

SCHOOL-TO-WORK TRANSITION; FOREIGN EXPERIENCE

James Bryant Conant, former president of Harvard University, commented some years ago on the role of education not only in directing youths to areas of employment where demand exists, but also in facilitating their changeover from school to work: "The educational experiences of youth should fit their subsequent employment. There should be a smooth transition from full-time schooling to a full-time job, whether the transition be after grade 10 or after graduation from high school, college, or university." [8]

A serious disparity exists between the ideal transition mentioned by Conant and the actuality. A Cornell University sociologist has written: "One of the most definitive characteristics of the occupational nature of the urbanized society is the conspicuous absence of apparent mechanisms for communicating occupational knowledge and equating occupations with interests and abilities." [9] The 1968 Manpower Report of the President to Congress outlined the deficiencies as follows:

> Eight of 10 school dropouts have never had counseling by school or employment office officials about training or employment opportunities, and 4 out of 10 high school graduates have never had such counseling. There are no school counselors at all in 13 per cent of the nation's secondary schools and in 90 per cent of its elementary schools. . . . Even smaller proportions have been exposed to supervised work experience while in school. Among out-of-school youth in

[8] James Bryant Conant, *Slums and Suburbs* (1961), p. 40.
[9] Lee Taylor, *Occupational Sociology* (1968), p. 189.

175

COMPARISON OF UNEMPLOYMENT RATES

(Ratio of unemployment rate for youths in two age groups
to unemployment rate for persons aged 25 years or over)

	Aged 15 to 19	Aged 20 to 24
United States	5.00*	2.19
Italy	4.48	3.13
France	3.71	1.41
Sweden	2.60	1.27
Japan	2.14	1.43

* Unemployment rate in this case, for example, is five times as great as that among
workers aged 25 or over.

SOURCE: Franz A. Groemping, *Transition From School to Work in Selected Countries* (1969), p. 34.

1963, only 7 per cent of high school graduates and 3 per cent of
dropouts had such work experience.

Numerous books and pamphlets describing the various
occupations are available, but "The existing career literature
is uniformly sloppy," in the opinion of Peter M. Sandman,
author of *Unabashed Career Guide.*[10] Books and materials
on specific occupations, Sandman found, stress only the attractive aspects of each occupation. The U. S. Department of
Labor, however, attempts to present balanced descriptions in
its *Occupational Outlook Handbook* (1968).

Youths in Western Europe and Japan have much less difficulty than American youths in crossing the bridge from
school to work, as indicated in the accompanying table. The
smoother school-work transition in the places mentioned is
due in part to the prevalence there of a number of work-
oriented practices. Among these practices are early exposure
of school children to varieties of work, through visits and
school-supervised work assignments; extensive vocational
counseling; enrollment of students, upon completion of their
compulsory schooling, in public vocational training programs
or an apprenticeship; flexible administration of vocational
schools, with adaptations to technological change; and financial help from the government for apprenticeship or on-the-
job training.

Herbert Bienstock, a Department of Labor official, commented recently on the superiority of foreign vocational
guidance. "It is a strange paradox," he wrote, "that in other
nations, where the social and economic institutions are less
complex than in the United States, we find the vocational

---

[10] Quoted in *Careers Today*, February 1969, p. 62.

guidance arts to be more highly developed. It would seem that the reverse would—and surely should—be true." [11]

Not all of the methods used abroad in facilitating the transition from school to work are applicable in the United States. For one thing, vocational training in foreign countries reflects, as the President's 1968 Manpower Report stated, "a heavily structured status system for entry into jobs—the kind of system that has been traditionally rejected in the United States." Nevertheless, the shortage in the United States of skilled mechanics and repairmen has been due in part to a mistake not generally made by the Europeans. Philip H. Abelson, editor of *Science*, wrote in the issue of Aug. 16, 1968: "One of our greatest mistakes has been to accord special prestige to a college degree while displaying indifference toward quality in craftsmanship. We reward verbal skill and abstract reasoning and deny dignity to manual workers."

Evolution of Today's Job Structure

THIS COUNTRY, from colonial times to about 1870, was primarily an agricultural society. The principal economic activities were farming, forestry, the fur trade, and fisheries (including whaling). In 1800, more than nine-tenths of the American people made at least a part of their living from farming. Venturesome, literate, and ingenious farmers brought large areas under cultivation. The number of square miles of new farmland added to the total rose steadily from 65,000 in the decade of the 1790s to 215,000 in the 1840s. Farming was the occupation of nearly two-thirds of working Americans in 1850.

American farmers differed from Old World peasants in being mentally energetic, mobile, and eager to adopt new methods. The impact of technology on farming as an occupation began early in American history. Eli Whitney's invention in 1793 of the cotton gin, a device for separating fiber from seed, more than trebled the amount of cotton that could be processed in a day. Chiefly as a result of Whitney's invention, the American cotton crop increased from 1.5 million

---

[11] Herbert Bienstock, "The Transition to Work Here and Abroad: Do U. S. Youth Fare Worse?" *New Generation,* Winter 1969, p. 5.

pounds in 1790 to 85 million pounds in 1810. The cotton gin also stimulated extension of the plantation system and Negro slavery in the South. The individualistic, frontier-pushing farmer sought his fortune in the mid-West and the West rather than the South.

To provide training for the sons of American farmers, Rep. Justin S. Morrill (Whig Vt.) introduced in 1857 the first bill providing for state-administered land-grant colleges. The bill failed to pass. After several further attempts, Morrill's initiative finally led to the enactment, July 2, 1862, of a law donating extensive public lands to the states and territories for establishment of colleges. In the words of the law, "the leading object" of the land-grant colleges "shall be, without excluding other scientific and classical studies, and including military tactics, to teach such branches of learning as are related to agriculture and the mechanic arts, in such manner as the legislatures of the states may respectively prescribe, in order to promote the liberal and practical education of the industrial classes in the several pursuits and professions in life."

RISE OF EMPLOYMENT IN INDUSTRY AND SERVICES

The opening of vast areas to farming paved the way for growth of large urban centers of trade and industry in the mid-West and the West, while the industrial revolution was causing rapid expansion of cities in the East and the South. About the time of the Civil War and immediately thereafter, the rate of introduction of new inventions rose markedly, and projects to exploit hitherto unused natural resources also showed notable increases. Numerous companies were formed in the post-bellum period to develop petroleum, aluminum, steel, and the use of electricity. The proportion of jobs in farming declined to 40 per cent in 1900 and plummeted thereafter to about 4.3 per cent in 1969. From about 1900, the absolute number of farm jobs also fell off gradually.

The proportion of American workers engaged in production of goods (agriculture and industry combined) rose steadily until about 1950 but has since declined. Thus, just as agriculture over a period of decades gave way to industry (including mining and construction), so industry began about mid-century to give way to government, education, and other white-collar or service functions.

Jobs for the Future

DISTRIBUTION OF THE LABOR FORCE

(per cent)

	About 1910	About 1930	About 1950	About 1962
United States				
Agriculture	31	22	12	9
Industry	31	31	35	33
Service	38	47	53	59
United Kingdom				
Agriculture	12	6	5	4
Industry	43	43	47	48
Service	45	51	48	48
Germany				
Agriculture	34	29	23	14
Industry	26	30	33	38
Service	26	30	33	38

SOURCE: *International Encyclopedia of the Social Sciences* (1968), Vol. 5, p. 50.

That the United States is not unique in the move to service occupations is shown in the accompanying table comparing distribution of the labor force in this country and in two West European countries. Leon Greenberg, of the U. S. Bureau of Labor Statistics, doubts that the trend to service occupations will accelerate. He told an international conference on automation, at Oberhausen, Germany, in March 1968: "Employment in service producing industries as a per cent of total employment has risen about 3 percentage points every five years since 1947. . . . Projections indicate that the average five-year rise to 1975 will be slightly less—about 2.5 points." These projections suggest, Greenberg concluded, "that we need not be concerned with an acceleration in the shift from goods to services, at least for the next 10 years."

JOB SECURITY AND IDEAL OF FULL EMPLOYMENT

Working in the right kind of job, a job that suits one's abilities, interests, and aspirations, is vitally important. At times, however, it is even more important just to have a job—some way to earn a living. European governments early in the present century began to provide financial assistance to persons who had trouble in finding a job. In the United States, provision for unemployment insurance was made for the first time in the Social Security Act of 1935. That act became law in a year when 20 per cent of the labor force was without work.[12] As recently as July 9, 1969, President Nixon asked Congress to extend unemployment insurance to the

---

[12] See "Unemployment Benefits in Times of Prosperity," *E.R.R.*, 1965 Vol. I, pp. 163-164.

small proportion of workers still not covered—mainly workers in firms with only a handful of employees, nonprofit organizations, and state institutions.

Under the influence of Keynesian economics, the idea gained currency during the Great Depression of the 1930s that governments bore responsibility not only for providing subsistence payments to the unemployed, but also for so directing the economy that jobs would be plentiful. A report by Lord Beveridge in 1944, *Full Employment in a Free Society*, and the Employment Act adopted by Congress in February 1946 were milestones toward general acceptance of that idea. The U.N. General Assembly's Universal Declaration of Human Rights, Dec. 10, 1948, stated in Article 23: "Everyone has the right to work, to free choice of employment, to just and favorable conditions of work and to protection against unemployment."

PROGRAMS TO HELP THE DISADVANTAGED GET JOBS

More than 5 per cent of the American labor force was unemployed in 1960, but in the same year more than 10 per cent of nonwhites were out of work. Concern for impoverished Negroes, Puerto Ricans, and Mexican-Americans, with special regard to their high rate of unemployment, led to initiation by the federal government of a number of special job-training and work-experience programs. These programs helped hundreds of thousands of ghetto dwellers and others, but although the unemployment rate for all workers had fallen below 4 per cent by 1968, it was still twice as high for nonwhites.

The first programs aimed to help deprived groups to get jobs were established under the Manpower Development and Training Act of March 15, 1962. This act authorized expenditures by the government for training and employing youths 16 to 21 years of age and for upgrading the skills of those whose old skills had been left behind by technology.[13] During the 1968 presidential campaign, Richard M. Nixon criticized the administration of the act, pledged that he would introduce improvements, and proposed that a National Computer Job Bank be set up to match job openings with persons seeking employment, anywhere in the country. The Department of Labor in September 1969 contracted with a private organization to conduct a pilot program of computerized

---

[13] See Congressional Quarterly's *Congress and the Nation* (Vol. II 1969), pp. 737-743.

matching of unemployed persons with job vacancies, to be expanded if it proves effective.

As part of President Johnson's war on poverty, the Economic Opportunity Act of Aug. 20, 1964, sought to eliminate barriers to employment of disadvantaged persons through neighborhood-oriented and youth-oriented work-experience and training programs.[14] "Possibly the most imaginative development in the creation of job opportunities for the disadvantaged," according to Prof. Garth L. Mangum of George Washington University, "has been the concept of employing the poor to serve the poor in the Community Action Program." Under that program, some 40,000 low-income persons were "involved as teacher aides in education and day care activities, clerical aides, neighborhood aides who visit homes, bars and other places to reorient persons eligible for available services, counseling aides and employment aides who assist professionals in counseling, job development and placement."[15]

Future Changes in Employment Picture

NINE-TENTHS of the scientists and engineers who ever lived are alive today, according to a widely accepted estimate. They are enlarging the frontiers of understanding about man and his world, and developing techniques for manipulating nature, at a geometric rate of progression. As the discoveries and innovations of these creative minds proliferate, the knowledge explosion steadily erodes the theoretical education and the professional or technical skills of a generation of workers. Not only methods but also basic concepts are constantly being outdated and replaced by others.[16]

A study group established by the General Electric Co. in 1968 found that, after an initial period of formal education, "the process of learning and re-training is expected to continue throughout a person's career, leading to new programs and new relationships between business, unions, govern-

---

[14] *Ibid.*, p. 750.
[15] Garth L. Mangum, "Government as Employer of Last Resort," in Sar A. Levitan and others (eds.), *Towards Freedom from Want* (1968), p. 147.
[16] See "Retraining for New Jobs," *E.R.R.*, 1962 Vol. II, pp. 777-778.

ments, schools and universities to institutionalize this process." [17] Prof. James R. Bright of Harvard's Graduate School of Business Administration has warned that manual workers are not the only ones who will need refresher training:

> If technological advances are going to come more rapidly, be more severe, and differ widely from what has gone before, it follows that education and reeducation must take place at frequent intervals. The factory worker will need to be taught a new skill. The manager and engineer must acquire a working knowledge of new technology and analytical approaches.[18]

That the manager and the engineer will need to be particularly flexible is suggested by Auren Uris of the Research Institute of America. He has predicted: "In the business world of the future, experience will be a dirty word. In almost every case, a previous or 'old' way of doing things will be unacceptable." [19]

Some observers believe that new technology and changing social mores will require the average worker to change jobs more than once, perhaps several times, during his working life. Surprisingly, recent reports indicate that occasionally even scientists may need to learn a new trade. Reductions in federal programs of research and development during 1969 led Bryce Nelson to report that the job market in chemistry and other sciences was tightening. He wrote that "Unless the tendency to cut back on federal science spending is reversed, it may well be that the scientific profession will be winnowed to those able scientists who are driven primarily by love of their work." [20]

Nevertheless, it is expected there will be growing shortages of many types of personnel, especially in the professions, in the coming decade. Medical schools, noted the *Morgan Guaranty Survey* of November 1969, turn out about 9,000 doctors annually. This is only half of the number needed each year to keep up with health needs of a growing population that is expected to total 228 million by 1980—a gain of about 24 million above the U. S. population in 1969. The *Survey* added:

> Workers outside of the professions also will be in tight supply in the coming decade. Rebuilding urban areas of the nation alone would require an added 7,000 carpenters each year, yet in recent years the

17 General Electric Co., *Our Future Business Environment* (1968), p. 18.

18 James R. Bright, "Technology, Business, and Education," in Walter J. Ong (ed.), *Knowledge and the Future of Man; International Symposium* (1968), p. 211.

19 Auren Uris, "Executives of the Future," *Nation's Business*, January 1969, p. 69.

20 Bryce Nelson, "A Surplus of Scientists? The Job Market Is Tightening," *Science*, Oct. 31, 1969, p. 582.

number of carpenters in the U.S. has actually declined by 50,000, according to one manpower study. Even unskilled laborers are expected to be increasingly scarce in most areas of the country as industry and government training programs steadily reduce the "hard core" unemployed. From all indications, the do-it-yourself trend for the American homeowner is not to disappear in the seventies.

Labor-force growth in the 1970s is expected to increase at a 1.7 per cent annual rate, slightly higher than the indicated growth rate of 1.6 per cent for the decade of the sixties.

EFFECTS OF AUTOMATION ON ATTITUDE OF WORKERS

In old and new locations, personnel managers and other administrators are devoting increased attention to the satisfaction or dissatisfaction which the jobs in their establishments provide for the intellectual and manual workers there. In a labor market in which advanced skills are in short supply, employers are eager to husband the loyalty of their most capable workers. In this connection, the feeling is growing that to the greatest possible extent jobs should be fitted to individual talents; that is, that the work to be done should be structured in accordance with the interests and aptitudes of the workers, as against the older idea that jobs are what they are, and the only problem of placement is to find a round peg for a round hole.

Michael Silva, discussing the impact of tomorrow's college graduate on the world of business, has written: "A new wave of Americans, with more affluence and education than ever before, will be creating their own jobs in large companies instead of filling slots as many do today. With necessities like food and fun assured as a right, the post-affluents will demand and get careers free of slavishness, and do work that is more like play." [21] A 1969 survey of recruiters for business concerns indicated that college graduates today appear less concerned with income than with other job satisfactions, including company participation in community affairs and public service.[22] The director of manpower utilization of the American Telephone & Telegraph Co. jestingly envisions workers "picketing their employer with placards that read: We demand meaningful work. We want to be plugged in. We demand responsibility." [23]

---

[21] Michael Silva, "The Mass Elite," *Careers Today*, Charter Issue, 1968, p. 80.

[22] "Amid Campus Unrest, Graduates Rush for Jobs," *U.S. News and World Report*, April 7, 1969, pp. 49-51.

[23] Robert N. Ford, "The Obstinate Employee," *Psychology Today*, November 1969, p. 33.

ments, schools and universities to institutionalize this process." [17] Prof. James R. Bright of Harvard's Graduate School
of Business Administration has warned that manual workers
are not the only ones who will need refresher training:

> If technological advances are going to come more rapidly, be more
> severe, and differ widely from what has gone before, it follows that
> education and reeducation must take place at frequent intervals. The
> factory worker will need to be taught a new skill. The manager and
> engineer must acquire a working knowledge of new technology and
> analytical approaches. [18]

That the manager and the engineer will need to be particularly flexible is suggested by Auren Uris of the Research
Institute of America. He has predicted: "In the business
world of the future, experience will be a dirty word. In almost every case, a previous or 'old' way of doing things will
be unacceptable." [19]

Some observers believe that new technology and changing
social mores will require the average worker to change jobs
more than once, perhaps several times, during his working
life. Surprisingly, recent reports indicate that occasionally
even scientists may need to learn a new trade. Reductions in
federal programs of research and development during 1969
led Bryce Nelson to report that the job market in chemistry
and other sciences was tightening. He wrote that "Unless the
tendency to cut back on federal science spending is reversed,
it may well be that the scientific profession will be winnowed
to those able scientists who are driven primarily by love of
their work." [20]

Nevertheless, it is expected there will be growing shortages of many types of personnel, especially in the professions,
in the coming decade. Medical schools, noted the *Morgan
Guaranty Survey* of November 1969, turn out about 9,000
doctors annually. This is only half of the number needed each
year to keep up with health needs of a growing population
that is expected to total 228 million by 1980—a gain of about
24 million above the U. S. population in 1969. The *Survey*
added:

> Workers outside of the professions also will be in tight supply in
> the coming decade. Rebuilding urban areas of the nation alone would
> require an added 7,000 carpenters each year, yet in recent years the

---

[17] General Electric Co., *Our Future Business Environment* (1968), p. 18.

[18] James R. Bright, "Technology, Business, and Education," in Walter J. Ong (ed.),
Knowledge and the Future of Man; International Symposium (1968), p. 211.

[19] Auren Uris, "Executives of the Future," *Nation's Business*, January 1969, p. 69.

[20] Bryce Nelson, "A Surplus of Scientists? The Job Market Is Tightening," *Science*,
Oct. 31, 1969, p. 582.

number of carpenters in the U. S. has actually declined by 50,000, according to one manpower study. Even unskilled laborers are expected to be increasingly scarce in most areas of the country as industry and government training programs steadily reduce the "hard core" unemployed. From all indications, the do-it-yourself trend for the American homeowner is not to disappear in the seventies.

Labor-force growth in the 1970s is expected to increase at a 1.7 per cent annual rate, slightly higher than the indicated growth rate of 1.6 per cent for the decade of the sixties.

EFFECTS OF AUTOMATION ON ATTITUDE OF WORKERS

In old and new locations, personnel managers and other administrators are devoting increased attention to the satisfaction or dissatisfaction which the jobs in their establishments provide for the intellectual and manual workers there. In a labor market in which advanced skills are in short supply, employers are eager to husband the loyalty of their most capable workers. In this connection, the feeling is growing that to the greatest possible extent jobs should be fitted to individual talents; that is, that the work to be done should be structured in accordance with the interests and aptitudes of the workers, as against the older idea that jobs are what they are, and the only problem of placement is to find a round peg for a round hole.

Michael Silva, discussing the impact of tomorrow's college graduate on the world of business, has written: "A new wave of Americans, with more affluence and education than ever before, will be creating their own jobs in large companies instead of filling slots as many do today. With necessities like food and fun assured as a right, the post-affluents will demand and get careers free of slavishness, and do work that is more like play." [21] A 1969 survey of recruiters for business concerns indicated that college graduates today appear less concerned with income than with other job satisfactions, including company participation in community affairs and public service.[22] The director of manpower utilization of the American Telephone & Telegraph Co. jestingly envisions workers "picketing their employer with placards that read: We demand meaningful work. We want to be plugged in. We demand responsibility." [23]

[21] Michael Silva, "The Mass Elite," *Careers Today*, Charter Issue, 1968, p. 80.

[22] "Amid Campus Unrest, Graduates Rush for Jobs," *U. S. News and World Report*, April 7, 1969, pp. 49-51.

[23] Robert N. Ford, "The Obstinate Employee," *Psychology Today*, November 1969, p. 33.

Investigators have found that, in an office or shop where the work has been computerized, the new situation contains elements of both increased and decreased satisfaction for the workers. Machines have taken over the tasks which are less pleasant and more strenuous; workers tend to have greater physical mobility on the job and more frequent contact with the technical staff; and there is often increased opportunity for exercise of judgment. Counterbalancing these advantages are the faster tempo, lack of control over the pace of the work, necessity for constant alertness and close concentration, and the heavy burden of responsibility imposed by awareness of the serious consequences of an error. Sometimes boredom also is in evidence.

NEW CONCEPTS OF WORK, LEISURE, AND CREATIVITY

Experts are not agreed on how soon, if ever, society will be able to turn over most of its work to machines. Arnold J. Toynbee is confident that such a time will come. "The accelerating advance of technology is carrying us towards a novel state of society," he has said. "We are all going to be paid high wages for working for only a few hours in the week." [24] Kent D. Shinbach, an American medical researcher, has ventured a time estimate:

> Within 40 years only one-fourth of the population will be involved in what we now call work. And this involvement will usually amount to a 24-hour work week. . . . Jobs and workers will eventually be known as outmoded concepts from our mechanical heritage. . . . All of us who anticipate, cherish, and celebrate the weekend are probably among the last adherents of a fading cult. [25]

Joseph N. Froomkin and others hold a different view: "The prospects of a utopia, or a Calvinist hell, where work will become redundant, are not likely to face Western society in the near future. Historically, periods of increases in productivity have been followed by periods of stagnation in the rate of increase in productivity." [26] According to Peter F. Drucker, "The report of the demise of work is not only premature; it is false. Indeed the trend runs the other way. Work is growing faster than the work force and is likely to continue to grow faster." [27]

---

[24] Arnold J. Toynbee, *Change and Habit; The Challenge of Our Times* (1966), p. 218.

[25] Kent D. Shinbach, "Technology and Social Change: Choosing a Near Future," *Mental Hygiene*, April 1968, p. 281.

[26] Joseph N. Froomkin (Department of Health, Education, and Welfare), "Automation," in the *International Encyclopedia of the Social Sciences* (1968), Vol. I, p. 487.

[27] Peter F. Drucker, "Worker and Work in the Metropolis," *Daedalus*, Fall 1968, p. 1243.

Jobs for the Future

A manpower study by the National Planning Association indicates that to achieve national goals would require by 1975 the employment of 10 million more persons than are expected to be in the labor force at that time.[28] Analysts in the Bureau of Labor Statistics also doubt that any trend toward drastic reduction of the world's work has begun. That planners and administrators at least will have more work to do in the future than they do now, is suggested by a summary of recent literature on technology and work which noted that, according to most predictions, "while workers will increasingly have free time, the upper echelons will not."[29]

The so-called Puritan concept considers work as unavoidable and arduous, as a duty, and as dealing with things. A comparable idea, that work is necessary for the normal functioning of human beings, was held by Sigmund Freud. A recent student of the subject pointed out:

> The most important function of work is to enable us to use our capacities to the full. Aristotle, over 2,000 years ago, pinpointed the issue with unparalleled clarity. The essence of happiness, he argued, is doing the best we can with the talents we have. . . . People will have to discover personal or social goals which they feel worthy of serious effort. This will require new attitudes, and education will have to create them.[30]

While many statesmen and economists are striving to find ways of increasing paid employment and thus reducing unemployment, Robert Theobald feels that society has an obligation to promote, through applications of technology, the fullest amount of unemployment—that is, freedom from the necessity for regular, prolonged periods of work. Theobald asserts that society should, at the same time, develop "financial mechanisms that enable the individual to act as an institution, self-directed, and alone responsible for his activities." Schools and universities should "develop creativity and enlarge the capacity of the individual to think in terms of his own uniqueness."[31]

The human race itself, Victor C. Ferkiss believes, is "on the threshold of self-transfiguration, of attaining new powers over itself and its environment that can alter its nature as fundamentally as walking upright or the use of tools."[32]

---

[28] Leonard A. Lecht, *Manpower Needs for National Goals in the 1970s* (1969).

[29] Harvard University Program on Technology and Society, *Technology and Work* (Winter 1969), p. 8.

[30] Hans P. Rickman, *Living With Technology* (1967), pp. 84-85, 90.

[31] Robert Theobald, "Should Men Compete With Machines?" *The Nation*, May 9, 1966, pp. 546, 548.

[32] Victor C. Ferkiss, *Technological Man: The Myth and the Reality* (1969), p. 6.

187

Ferkiss views the American astronauts as forerunners of this new, creative species, "technological man." In the dawning civilization which he envisions, semi-skilled and unskilled labor might still play a large part in the economy but have little share in the job satisfactions afforded the scientific elite. Pursuits which observers believe likely to play an important role in the future organization of work and leisure include voluntary study, artistic creation, and religion.[33]

INDIVIDUAL FREEDOM AND PLANS FOR MANPOWER USE

For the near future, when work for pay will still be an urgent reality, social theorists face the problem of trying to harmonize manpower planning and individual freedom. Eli Ginzberg of Columbia University has highlighted the problem:

> There is an inherent antagonism between placing high value on the freedom of the individual to choose his work and to select his employer and the thrust of manpower planning which aims at influencing, even directing, the choices that people make about their future occupations and the decisions they reach about current employment.... But we know that one man's freedom may be another's fetters. . . . [For example, in declining employment areas such as agriculture,] if nothing is done to help the young, freedom may prove to be, as in Anatole France's parable, only the freedom to go hungry.[34]

Several kinds of governmental action affecting manpower have come to be regarded as consistent with individual freedom. Among them are stimulation of job-producing business expansion through loans or special tax incentives and through increases of consumer purchasing power in the form of higher social security payments or lower taxes; provision of opportunities for vocational training and of funds for subsistence while undergoing training; and expenditures for public works to provide jobs as well as to serve other social purposes.

Some economists favor, as a job-producing measure, substantial reduction of the over-all length of time worked by members of the labor force—through extension of schooling, shortening of the work-week, lengthening of vacations, and early retirement. Simple reduction of the work-week has been ineffectual in the past as a device to increase jobs, for employers often have preferred to pay current employees at

---

[33] See "Leisure in the Great Society," *E.R.R.*, 1964 Vol. II, pp. 914-919.

[34] Eli Ginzberg, *Manpower Agenda for America* (1968), p. 242.

overtime rates rather than to hire additional workers. Furthermore, when the work-week is shortened, some workers take on second jobs.

Edwin F. Shelley, president of an engineering firm, has suggested "a national system of Earned Educational Leave," adjustable to the rate of unemployment. Thus, if 5 per cent of the workers were unemployed, he would remove 5 per cent of the labor force for a year, "for refreshment of skills, knowledge, and personal outlook"; if 10 per cent were unemployed, a like percentage would be assigned to educational leave; and so forth, with financing of the costs shared by business and government.[35]

Individual freedom is not infringed upon by government correlation of information about areas of declining or rising demand and supply or by provision of guidance and other forms of assistance to bring jobs and workers together. In all such programs, it is important for organs of government to avoid the opposite evils—the Scylla and Charybdis—of (1) overzealously requiring people to choose, prepare for, and work at jobs arbitrarily determined to be appropriate, and (2) inadequately guiding, advising, and assisting persons who are, or will be, in the market for jobs. In looking ahead into the decade of the 1970s one observation can be made with safety: the jobs that pay the best and are the most satisfying will go to those who are best prepared by reason of education and training.

---

[35] Edwin F. Shelley, "Earned Educational Leave: A Proposal," in Juanita M. Kreps (ed.), *Technology, Manpower, and Retirement Policy* (1966), pp. 193-194.